David Friedrich Strauss, Hermann Ulrici

Strauss as a Philosophical Thinker

A review of his book

David Friedrich Strauss, Hermann Ulrici

Strauss as a Philosophical Thinker
A review of his book

ISBN/EAN: 9783337068462

Printed in Europe, USA, Canada, Australia, Japan

Cover: Foto ©Thomas Meinert / pixelio.de

More available books at **www.hansebooks.com**

STRAUSS AS A PHILOSOPHICAL THINKER.

A REVIEW

OF HIS BOOK,

"THE OLD FAITH AND THE NEW FAITH,"

AND

A CONFUTATION OF ITS MATERIALISTIC VIEWS.

BY

HERMANN ULRICI.

TRANSLATED, WITH AN INTRODUCTION,

BY

CHARLES P. KRAUTH, D.D.,
VICE-PROVOST OF THE UNIVERSITY OF PENNSYLVANIA.

PHILADELPHIA:
SMITH, ENGLISH & CO.,
710 ARCH STREET.
EDINBURGH: T. & T. CLARK.
1874.

Entered according to Act of Congress, in the year 1874,

By SMITH, ENGLISH & CO.,

In the Office of the Librarian of Congress, at Washington, D. C.

PHILADELPHIA:
SHERMAN & CO., PRINTERS.

CONTENTS.

INTRODUCTION: PAGE
   The Materialism of our Day, ... 9
   Aim of the Present Discussion, ... 13
   Importance of the Question, ... 14
   The Problem of the Hour, ... 21
   The Materialistic Physicists, ... 22
   Materialism a Power in our Day, ... 25
   Necessity of Discussing Materialism, . . . 27
   Recent Discussions—Appearance of Strauss's Book, 31
   Strauss's Reviewers, ... 35
   Points of Interest in the Reviews of Strauss, . 39
   Strauss's Inconsistency with his Earlier Position, . 49
   The Great Physicists, ... 51
   Mischievous Tendencies of Strauss's Book, . . 58
   The Political Elements in Strauss, . . . 63
   The Reactionary Tendency of Strauss's Book, . 65
   Ulrici's Review of Strauss, ... 67

ULRICI'S REVIEW OF STRAUSS:
   I. Strauss considered as a Philosophical Thinker, 73
   II. What Strauss proposes in "The New Faith and the Old Faith:" his real aim the Destruction of the Old Faith, . . . 75
   III. "Are we still Christians?". . . . 78
   IV. "Have we Religion still?" 79
   V. Strauss's Theory of the Rise of Religion, . 84
   VI. Strauss's Repudiation of the Argument for the Existence of God, ... 86

		PAGE
VII.	Immortality of the Soul,	91
VIII.	The Essential Nature of Religion,	92
IX.	The Permanent in Religion—Man and the Universe,	95
X.	The New Faith,	98
XI.	The Discovery,	100
XII.	The Good and the Bad,	104
XIII.	Strauss in Conflict with consistent Materialism; Pessimism; Schopenhauer; Von Hartmann,	106
XIV.	"What is our Apprehension of the Universe?"	108
XV.	The Cosmogony of Kant and La Place,	113
XVI.	Origin of Life upon Earth—Generatio Æquivoca—Organic and Inorganic,	115
XVII.	Origin of Species—The Darwinian Theory,	120
XVIII.	The Ape and Man—Man and the Animals, their Affinities and Distinctions,	125
XIX.	The Soul,	128
XX.	Strauss's Appeal to Du Bois-Reymond,	133
XXI.	The Notion of Design in the Light of Natural Science—Philosophy of the Unconscious,	137
XXII.	The setting aside of the Doctrine of Final Causes in Nature by Darwin,	139
XXIII.	"How shall we Order our Life?"	144
XXIV.	The Primary Principle of Morality,	146
XXV.	Strauss's attempt to show that he does not hold that the Universe is a thing of Chance,	152
XXVI.	Nature coming to Self-recognition,	155
XXVII.	Strauss's direct Contradiction of himself,	158
XXVIII.	Strauss's Ideal Strivings—His Recognition of Mystery,	160
XXIX.	Conclusion—The New Philosophy,	162

INTRODUCTION.

THE MATERIALISM OF OUR DAY.

To any reader who knows the vast range of topics involved in a complete discussion of Materialism, the very dimensions of the volume he holds in his hand would show that it proposes to touch upon no more than a part of a part of that vast theme. For the questions of Materialism cover the physical, intellectual and moral universe. There is nothing deep or high in man's life, or thinking, in his present or his future, which they do not in some measure condition. Materialism calls for an obliteration of what is noblest in the past, the abandonment of our richest heritages, and a total reconstruction of all the present, an abrupt change in all that tended to a future with roots deepset in the past. If Materialism be successful in establishing its claim, it will involve the greatest revolution which has ever taken place in the world. To make this volume a complete summary, not to say, a survey of all the facts and principles which are covered by the assertion and exposure of such a system as Materialism, would involve the compression of a world to the dimensions of a pea. All sciences have been made tributary to the false assumptions of the Materialism of our day, and all the sciences would have to be laid under contribution to furnish the refutation of it. Here, as everywhere the great corrective of abuse is the restoration of the right use. The fact that the abuse of science has been made to sustain Materialism is itself the best evidence that the right use of science will most completely overthrow Materialism. If so much science promotes Materialism, it is proof not that we need less science, but that we need more. So much more will undo the mischief which so much has done. Only let the science be real science, and there cannot be too much of it. To appeal from science in its legitimate sphere, to authority, in behalf of religion, is not to secure religion but to betray it. Science and Religion are occupied with two books, but both books are from one hand; in their true workings they are engaged in two parts of one great aim. Science moves ever toward the proof how supernatural is the natural; Religion moves toward the proof how natural is the supernatural. For nature in the narrower sense, is in her spring, Supernatural. To this point all natural science constantly advances. The more problems natural science settles the more it raises; the more it diminishes the sphere in which the speculation of the past found its range, the more does it enlarge the sphere of the future speculation. Ours is at once the age of the supremest affluence in questions solved, and of the most pressing poverty in questions opened and unanswered. A question settled is a question planted, and green, young questions spring all around it. The more we know of Nature, the more cogent becomes the necessity of the Supernatural. On the other hand, the Supernatural is within Nature, in Nature's broader sense. In this sense Nature is identical with the real. Everything is Nature that is not non-nature; everything is natural that is not unnatural. The Supernatural is not to be construed as the contranatural, but as the natural itself in its supremest sphere, and God and His directest works are supernatural because they are by pre-eminence natural. In this sense Nature is not a conception embraced in the conception of God, but as all-embracing, most of all embraces God as the Supreme Nature, whose most supernatural works, are, as such, most natural. The sciences which represent nature, and the faith to which are committed the oracles of the Supernatural, must in proportion as they prove true to themselves, prove true to each other. Whatever may be the apparent difference of their origin, though the one seem to spring out of the earth, the other to look down from heaven, knowledge and faith shall at last meet together and kiss each other. It is a common canon of science and religion to "judge nothing before the time," and yet it is the neglect of this canon on both sides which has been the occasion of their most serious misunderstandings and of their sharpest collisions. Some who have professed to represent science, have been too ready with their theories, and some who have claimed to be special defenders of the faith have been too absolute in their interpretations, and it is precisely between provisional dogmatical theories, and provisional dogmatic interpretations, the severest conflict has taken place. It has been a battle of guesses. The warfare will ultimately be laid by the overthrow of the hasty theory, or of the hasty interpretation, or of both.

AIM OF THE PRESENT DISCUSSION.

Fully to discuss Materialism, which assumes to be the philosophy of all knowledge, would involve in the nature of the case a presentation of an immense body of facts, drawn from the intellectual and moral sciences. Simply to state the misstatements of Materialism without correcting them, or to give its arguments without answering them, would demand a series of elaborate and ponderous volumes. And yet this little volume, meant for the fireside and the pocket, is large enough and rich enough, to give both sides of this great question, in the words of very able representatives of both. It is sufficiently comprehensive at least to help the reader to test what Materialism is made of, and to settle the question whether we are willing to have the edifice of our convictions built of it. In our schoolday Greek reading, under the painful embarrassment with which a grammar and dictionary invest the ordinarily spontaneous process of laughing, we were taught to laugh at the Scholastikos, the Greek Irishman, who having a house to sell, carried around a brick as a specimen of it. But the Scholastikos, as the Irishman not unfrequently is, was perhaps wiser than some who laughed at him. The brick settled at least one question, and in settling that, settled to many a man all the other questions. To the man who wanted a house of marble, the brick settled it, that the house of whose material it was a specimen was not the house he wanted. This volume carries with it, both in the statements of STRAUSS, which are given in his own words, and in the replies of ULRICI, enough evidence to decide what Materialism is. It shows in that very world of scientific fact and of speculative thought in which Materialism is most boastful and arrogant, how little it has to tempt the thoughtful man to forego the use of logical reason, how little to justify the good man in doing violence to his moral sense. It shows that sunbaked mud bricks, all the weaker for the shining particles glittering in them, compose the building with which Materialism proposes to replace the edifice of human convictions and faiths, which have stood unmoved through the storms of age.

IMPORTANCE OF THE QUESTION.

It is impossible for the thinkers of our day to look with indifference on its materialistic tendencies. If views of this class possess, in them-

IMPORTANCE OF THE QUESTION. 15

selves, little philosophical importance, they yet have a claim on our attention, not only because of the great mischief they may produce, but also because they are bearing a part in widening and intensifying that general interest in the natural sciences, of which they are in part the effect, in part the cause. All the intensest passions of our human life gather about some sort of battle. The unfought is unfelt. The materialistic struggle more than anything else vitalizes the natural sciences—for thinking is, after all, the supremest pleasure of thinking man. The intellectual beats the material in all long races. In the struggle which Materialism has produced, germs have been scattered, and are already springing, which sooner or later will modify in important respects the philosophy of the future. The influence of the natural sciences in the sphere of philosophy is more marked in our own day than at any period since ARISTOTLE, Master of Physics and Master of Metaphysics, laid in the one the basis of the other. Our age pays, not for the first time, the greatest of tributes received by that wonderful man—the tribute of denouncing him and his method, meaning neither the real Aristotle, nor the real Aristotelian method, and then following more closely than before in the real walk of the great Peripatetic. Ours is an Aristotelian age.

In one respect, indeed, these last days of philosophy tend in a dangerous respect to be like its very first—to make Physics everything and Metaphysics nothing. But the difference is nevertheless marked, between the earliest and latest eras. Physical observation, in our day, has developed into science; all the departments of the natural sciences have been immensely enriched, and some of the most brilliant discoveries of all time have been made.

This has naturally led to a predominance of that class of interests over every other. Ours is the era of the physical sciences, and of their tributaries and applications. These have thrown into the shade all the other departments of human thought. Not even civil and political issues have excited the interest in the intellectual world which is excited by the great physicists. Our poets, statesmen and soldiers have not given to us a household name more frequently on our lips than that of AGASSIZ. No Englishmen are spoken of more than DARWIN and TYNDALL; and HUMBOLDT, LOTZE, HELMHOLTZ, and a host of others, shine with peculiar splendor in the great galaxy of the Germany of our age.

It is, however, especially the philosophical sciences which have been injured by the predominance of physical studies, when these studies have assumed the unnatural position, not of presupposition to the metaphysical, a place which is rightly their due, but of antagonism to it. Physical science seems, indeed, to furnish a strong contrast to Metaphysics; the one seems so fruitful a field, the other so barren an arena; the one claims the power of enforcing conviction of its facts on every intelligent mind, the other is apparently incapable of healing the divisions it originates. The physical sciences seem so useful in everyday life, going down to the heart of the world to warm and enrich us, and challenging clouds and stars to help the husbandman and the sailor. In contrast with them the metaphysical sciences seem so attenuated, so utterly vague! Mills do not grind, nor engines labor at their command. They do not put fruits upon our tables, nor fill our fields with springing grass for our herds. This contrast becomes the more specious and more unfavorable to Metaphysics, because few comparatively have a clear conception of the relation of the physical and the intellectual sciences. Where a comparison is made, it is often made between the highest forms of the physical sciences, and the weakest and most extravagant forms of metaphysical speculation. We are asked to look upon the picture of some Hyperion of the one, by the side of some Satyr of the other. Those who know the facts, know that the philosophical spirit is the spirit which vitalizes all the material with the mental, and connects all phenomena with conceptions of the essence they represent, all facts with truth, all effects with causes, all that is individual with the coherence of relations, all premises with inferences, all the transient with the ultimate. They know that it is the spirit which lays the whole realm of nature under tribute, and that without this spirit, and the results of its life in men, and its labor for men, we should have no natural sciences. It is imminent in them even when they know it not; its death would be their death. It is the life-unit of the coral-bed of the accretions of physics. The physical sciences are but one efflorescence, among the innumerable forms in which the philosophical spirit reveals itself. All the physical sciences, as sciences, rest upon metaphysical data, and develop themselves toward metaphysical sequences. The intensest interest of cultivated minds, in the very sphere of what seems most like unrelievable physics, turns toward the theory, the hypothesis, the speculation it involves. Without the metaphysical spirit, the chemist sinks to the condition of the other compound substances of his laboratory; the astronomer is but a big child playing with a big Orrery; the geologist possesses the penetration of an artesian auger—no more. Such men are but the tools of science, not its masters. The grand interest which attaches to modern science, is at its root an interest in the philosophy it involves. An author like LEWES writes a very charming book, the theory of whose theory is, that the metaphysical sciences are of no value, the theory of whose existence as an elaborate and favorite work of its author and of the public is, that the history of these valueless things has an enchantment of some supreme order for himself and them. But after LEWES has warned men from metaphysics, by the very inconsistent process of fascinating them with its history, he discovers that, after all, COMTE and the Positivist school to the contrary notwithstanding, man cannot live by bread alone. He has found that his own intellectual life could not endure the self-imposed starvation produced by abstinence from its true food. As the result of his larger experience, he makes a " change of front," and tries to cover his movement by masking it with the name of "Metempyrics." He has shown that even a very poor system of metaphysics is better than none, for LEWES's system is nothing more than the hoary, but not venerable, old Sensualism, with his hair dyed, and pantaloons substituted for knee-breeches.

Not only cannot the twin sciences be sundered, but they cannot bear healthfully a restriction of their vital intercommunication. To bind the ligament produces a fainting, which would be followed by death. It is therefore a shallow and ignorant impression, though sometimes cherished by men who ought to be ashamed to harbor it, that Philosophy in our day has played out its part, and that the best thing would be to hasten its absorption into physics and physiology. In this extravagant feeling and the sources of it, Materialism has found its account. The greatest representatives of Materialism have been, for the most part, physiologists and physicians, and from the same professional ranks have come some of its most thorough and vigorous assailants, for by a necessary law we look for the wildest errors, the most progressive truths, the soberest conservatism in the same general class of observers. Theological heresies originate with theologians, and so do the refutations of heresies. The clergy corrupt the Church—

they also reform it; and because physicians and physicists have done so much in producing Materialism, we look to physicians and physicists to do a great work in counteracting and healing it.

THE PROBLEM OF THE HOUR.

It is admitted that in scientific thinking the recent Materialism has scarcely brought in a single new idea. It has added nothing appreciable to LA METTRIE, DIDEROT, and VON HOLBACH. In fact, some of the theories passing as novelties in our own day, belong to a very remote antiquity. But this by no means proves that the Materialism of the hour has no significance in Philosophy. It sustains the old theories by a vast accumulation of new facts. The problem of the hour on one side is that Philosophy shall demonstrate its present harmony with the facts established by Physics, or failing to do this, shall adjust itself to them. On the other side, it is incumbent on the physical sciences to use their treasures and their advanced condition to aid in producing a philosophical system, in which the external world shall harmonize with the great metaphysical facts, for such facts there are, more certain than those of physics: on their certainty, indeed, all physical certainty depends. No part of the body of knowledge can say to another part, "I have no need of thee!"

The duty of aid and the necessity of harmony between these two great departments of knowledge has been profoundly felt by the ablest investigators of all time, and with increasing force to the present hour, in which the conviction culminates. No man can take the highest rank as a physicist or metaphysician, who is not both physicist and metaphysician. He is not of necessity equally both, but in whichever department he may be by pre-eminence, his greatness involves a thorough acquaintance with at least the results of the other. In the past, among the names that have intertwined both glories in one wreath, are the names of ARISTOTLE, DES CARTES, PASCAL, LEIBNITZ, KANT, SCHELLING, SCHALLER, and HEGEL. Among the living may be mentioned men like HELMHOLTZ, LOTZE, FICHTE, and ULRICI.

THE MATERIALISTIC PHYSICISTS.

The very roll-call of great names in the battle against Materialism shows how great is that battle, and how materialistic is our age. We see, indeed, very often assertions to the contrary. Sometimes they are made in pure ignorance by good people, whose happy little world is their fireside. Sometimes they are made in the blind polemical spirit which assumes that denial is disproof. Nevertheless it is true, this is a materialistic age. The progress of physical science, the splendor of recent discovery, the wonderful confirmation of the acutest conjectures of the past, the lustre of the names associated with these movements, have seemed to justify the physicists of our day in their exuberant triumph in the present achievements in the world of matter, and in their boundless assurance in regard to the future. No men have such prophetic souls as sanguine physicists. These theorists sometimes ask no more than a boundless past to justify their theories, or not unfrequently appeal, as if the gaze of the seer were granted them, to that happier future which is to furnish the missing links in the chain of demonstration. The sole reason that they cannot make out the theory of the present is, either that they cannot see quite far enough back into the past, or cannot see quite far enough into the future, except in the power of that theoretic faith which, disdaining such easy things as removing mountains, creates or uncreates universes at pleasure, and plays with nebulæ as boys play with marbles.

They utterly shame the believers in Revelation by the way in which *they* make faith the substance of things *hoped* for, and the evidence of things *not seen.*

Darwinism has simply to get far enough back to reach the ape of the past, to see him in the way of evolution to the man of the present, or to plunge deeply enough into the ages to come to see some man of the future evolved from an ape of the present—for we are primal to the future as the past is primal to us—and then the theory has a fact which fairly supports it—a something it does not possess to this hour. And as Darwinism needs but one of these two little things to make it an established theory, and as it has the boundless past to furnish one, the endless future to furnish the other—why, in a matter which may require hunting to all eternity, should we attempt to hurry these trusting adherents, in the production of this fact? If they wish to meet the debts of science by renewing its notes, they have many mercantile precedents for the method, which postpones the crash, even when it does not prevent it. If the enthusiast in the physical theories of the hour is willing to promise the bearskin before he has caught the bear, is not that a reason, in the judgment of charity, why we should pardon him if, in fact, he sometimes mistakes the promise of the skin *for* the actual possession of the bear, and that instead of considering the theory as a thing to be proven, he lays it down as a first principle by which everything known is to be explained, and in virtue of which everything desired is to be assumed?

MATERIALISM A POWER IN OUR DAY.

The lowest and the most practical of the characteristics of our day unite with some of its most brilliant and extravagant, to give to Materialism a special potency. In no land is the temptation, in some of its forms, greater than in our own, where material nature in her unsubdued majesty challenges man to conflict, or, in her fresh charms and munificent life, lures him to devotion. Materialism is popularized in our day. The magazines and papers are full of it. It creeps in everywhere, in the text-books, in school-books, in books for children, and in popular lectures. Materialism has entered into the great institutions of Germany, England, and America. Our old seats of orthodoxy have been invaded by it. New England, the storm-gauge of the rising thought of our land, begins to quiver on the edge of the coming hurricane.

The Materialism of our day is very versatile. It takes many shapes, often avoids a sharp conflict, assumes the raiment of light, knows how to play well the parts of free thought, truth, and beneficence. All the more securely does it pass in everywhere, so that we have Materialism intellectual, domestic, civil, philanthropic, and religious. Strangest of all, in a philosophical point of view, we have systems, like the system of SCHOPENHAUER, for example, which, under the form of the supremest Idealism, have the practical power of the lowest Materialism. Beginning in the sublimation of the spirit, they end by wallowing in the filthiest sty of the flesh.

Much of the Materialism of our day is servile and dogmatic, implicit in credulity, and insolent in assertion. Professing to be independent of names, and calling men to rally about the standard of absolute freedom from all authority, it parades names where it has names to parade, and vilifies the fair fame of those whom it cannot force into acquiescence or silence. Claiming to be free from partisanship, it is full of coarse intolerance. It is an inquisition, with such tortures as the spirit of our age still leaves possible. The *rabies theologorum* of which it loves to talk, pales before the *rabies physicorum* of this class, sometimes as directed against each other, yet more as directed against the men of science or of the church, who resist their theories. "If," says ERDMANN, "we are to "suppose that natural philosophy teaches us to "be dogmatic on topics about which we under-"stand nothing, then has natural philosophy "never found such zealous adepts as are found "among those who claim to be exact investiga-"tors. Anybody in our day who knows how "to handle a microscope, imagines that without "anything further, he can venture to be oracu-"lar on cause, condition, force, matter, logical "law, and truth."

NECESSITY OF DISCUSSING MATERIALISM.

These are a few of the indisputable facts which show that by pre-eminence Materialism is at once the greatest, both of the speculative and practical questions of the hour. Yet there are good and intelligent people who object even to an exposure of Materialism which may incidentally bring it to the notice of some, who they imagine, would apart from such an exposure, have remained in ignorance or indifference as to the whole subject. They think that these views, pernicious as they justly regard them, and indeed, because they do so regard them, should be kept completely out of sight wherever it is possible. It is quite possible that some may think that a knowledge of Ulrici's refutation is too dearly purchased by the knowledge of Strauss's errors which goes with it.

To such objections we answer, First: Ignorance is neither innocence nor safety. Knowledge, indeed, like all possessions, is capable of abuse. There is danger in whatever we do, and wherever there is danger in doing, there may be danger in leaving undone. There is danger of accident in exercise, there is the greater danger of loss of health in not exercising; there is the danger of choking, or of surfeiting in eating, the greater danger of starvation in not eating. Many men are drowned in swimming, many more men are drowned because they do not know how to swim. Hazard is the law of life, a law which becomes more exacting as life rises into its higher forms. Life itself binds up all hazards, and is itself the supreme hazard. He only never risks who never lives, and he who incurs none of the hazards of life performs none of its duties.

But if ignorance were innocence and safety, the features of our time on which we have dwelt, show that ignorance here is impossible. The choice is not between ignorance and some

NECESSITY OF DISCUSSING MATERIALISM. 29

sort of knowledge of Materialism, but between intelligent and correct impressions and false ones. Which shall the minds that are forming have: a knowledge of Materialism in all its strength, without the antidote, or of Materialism falsely understated, with the possibility, almost certainty, that they will one day see that it has been understated, and rush to the conclusion that its opponents did not dare to let the truth about it be known, or shall we have Materialism fairly presented and fairly met? If the last be the best course, then this volume meets a real want, for in it STRAUSS presents the plea for Materialism more attractively than it has ever been presented, and in it ULRICI annihilates that plea.

Especially is it the duty of educated men to know the grounds of the most dangerous and seductive error of our time, and to be master of the arguments by which that error is overthrown. The educated man ought to feel that without this knowledge he is not really educated. But if he be indifferent to it for himself, he should possess it for the benefit of others. No man liveth to himself, least of all the man of culture. He is of the class who are to be guides in their generation, and he must be willing to accept the responsibilities, and incur the risks of his vocation. The physician cannot heal contagious diseases without hazarding contagion. To the scholar and thinker others will come. The weakness of the thinker is the weakness of the seeker. The ignorance of the scholar is the hopeless ignorance of the learners, as, on the other hand, his knowledge will be their knowledge, his strength of assurance their conviction. It will to many be enough that he understands the problem, if they do not. The true scholar and thinker is, at last, the last power. In the world of thought the many decide, but the few decide the many. It is as in most free governments, the voters are a democracy, the rulers an aristocracy.

The mere seeming to avoid fair discussion, does more mischief than a real acquaintance with Materialism possibly can. To be cowardly is to be beaten without a battle. Materialism, with the arrogance common to all error, claims to be invincible. If it be not attacked, or its attack be declined, its explanation is invariably found, in the fears of its antagonists.

RECENT DISCUSSIONS. APPEARANCE OF STRAUSS'S BOOK.

The questions associated with Materialism have been discussed most earnestly and fully among the nations which may fairly claim the intellectual leadership of the world. England, France and America have names of renown on both sides of the question. Holland has thinkers whose contributions to this single department of thought, would reward the man who acquired its language solely to read them. It is in Germany, however, we find the treatment of these questions conducted with the most distinguished ability. Whether we ask for the most popular or the most profound works for Materialism, or against it, it is Germany which furnishes them. On the one side she has had FEUERBACH, MOLESCHOTT, BÜCHNER, and VOGT, as the chief advocates of Materialism; on the other SCHALLER, TITTMANN, FROHSCHAMMER, J. H. FICHTE, FABRI, BOHNER, and ULRICI, as its opponents, and now within a year past a host of able writers, old and new, has sprung to arms, on a new declaration of war.

This latest and sharpest struggle to which the Materialistic controversy has led is that in which the offensive was taken by DAVID FRIEDRICH

STRAUSS. The "great critic," as his friends loved to consider him, and as he loved to consider himself, brought to religion the sort of criticism which the Vandals brought to art, the criticism of barbarous, ruthless demolition, the savage iconoclasm, which spends its fury on the beauty it can neither comprehend nor feel. Among the secrets of STRAUSS's power has been that by skilful following he seemed to lead the tendencies of his time, that he wrote in a style admitted to be classic in form, and that he had a plausible superficiality, which made the indolent and half-informed reader satisfied that he saw to the bottom of the subject, because he saw to the bottom of the book. More than all he was indebted to a certain tempered extravagance, a power of fanaticism under a form of rationality. He gave himself with inexorable concentration in each case to a leading idea, never his own—he has not added a fact to knowledge nor a principle to speculation—and on this idea he has worked with a unity of aim, an industry of accumulation both of serviceable fact and illustration, which has made his presentation irresistible to many minds. That STRAUSS was at once so earnest and so cool, so much the moulder of the passions of others and the controller of his own, made him one of the great powers of his age. Essentially frivolous, both intellectually and ethically, he yet gives the reader an impression of earnestness and moral feeling, and thus influences those who, in the happy phrase of PHILIPPSON, "confound "the evidences of truthfulness with the evi-"dences of truth."

This man, not, we believe, without the order of Providence, came forth, in the evening of his long life, with a sort of summary, a canonical epitome, of the results of all his learning, and of all his speculation. It was the finality of a brilliant career, in which inordinate vanity had been wonderfully gratified. The man who had tried to shake all forms of religion, proposed, in his modesty, a compensation for them all in a discovery of his own. The great foe of all creeds, and most of all of the old creed, proposed a new creed, which was but an old creed, forgotten into newness. After trying to rob all men of their faith, he came forth with a confession of his own faith; a faith in which conscious matter reverenced and worshipped unconscious matter; in which reason bowed at the altar of the Unreason which had given it being; a faith without God or Providence, without spirit, freedom, or accountability; a faith devoid of a recognition of creation, redemption, or sanctification, of sin or of salvation. It had no heaven to desire, no hell to shun. Its last enemy is not death, but immortality; its goal is extinction. The only "Incarnation" of which it knows is "the Incarnation of the ape." Like the universe it imagined, this faith is uncreated and self-existent, an effect without a cause, a result without an antecedent, an end without aim, plan, design, or means. This is the "new faith" of STRAUSS, to which the new book is devoted. It is not wonderful that such a book from such a man attracted extraordinary attention, that it ran rapidly through a number of editions, and was eagerly read by thousands. It owed something to the virtues of its manner, its literary graces, its felicitous sophistries; it owed much more to the vices of its matter. A few came to its perusal in the hope of learning something; many took it up to find in it flattery for the convictions they already held. Most readers aimed at no more than the gratification of curiosity. The first class were bitterly disappointed; the second found that the sweetness of the flattery had some bitter qualifications; the last found the gratification they sought, for the book is really one of the strangest in the annals of Literature, and will be longest remembered as one of its curiosities.

STRAUSS'S REVIEWERS.

The intrinsic interest of the questions discussed, the antecedent general excitement of the public mind in regard to them, the greatness of STRAUSS's name, the marvellous success of his book in interesting men; and yet more, the audacious and dangerous character of its doctrines, the arrogance of its assertions, the Ultramontanism of its unbelief, and of its denunciation of doctrines in opposition to it,— STRAUSS was at once the Ecumenical Council of the " We," which proclaimed the dogma of the atheistic infallibility, and the Pio Nino who for the present embodied it—the boasts of independence in connection with the servility of its adhesions, the ultraisms of radicalism on which it built the ultraisms of conservatism, the all-destroying infidelity on which it reared its world-challenging highest faith—all these things led to an extraordinary number of notices of it. Scarcely one of them, even from the number of STRAUSS's warmest admirers, gave the book unmingled commendation. The great mass of notices coming from thinkers of various schools—Israelite and Christian, orthodox, rationalistic and old Catholic; from divines, men of science, philosophers and practical men—with a wonderful uniformity, condemned the principles of the book, exposed its falsities of argument and its errors in fact, and showed that all the moral relief which any of its better views offered, were in utter conflict with the fundamental principles of the speculations on which they professedly rested. Few books have attracted so many readers as STRAUSS's last book; very few have disappointed and disgusted so many.

Nothing, perhaps, could give a more vivid sense of the affluence of German learning, and the vigor of German thinking, than to notice what an amount of both has been called forth by this single book of STRAUSS. The catalogue of its literature would make a volume, and this literature, in some shape or other, takes in nearly every great question of the day, religious, literary, educational, philosophical, political and practical.

For reasons of various kinds, some of the reviewers of STRAUSS take a special prominence. MORITZ CARRIERE is distinguished as a historian of art, and a writer on æsthetics. HUBER, Professor of Philosophy in the University of Munich, KNOODT, ZIERNGEBL and MICHELIS, are "Old Catholics;" and it is a remarkable feature of the time that the "Old Catholics" have been represented with such special ability in the battle against STRAUSS.

Among philosophers by profession who have borne a part in the discussion may be mentioned IMMANUEL HERMANN FICHTE, who in his latest work, "The Theistic View of the World," has presented an account of the grand problems of the speculation of our day, with much that bears specially upon STRAUSS.

ALFRED DOVE is editor of the periodical "Im neuer Reich," and has won distinction as an essayist. DR. WEIS, the chemist, is author of "Antimaterialism," in which he has shown marked ability as an investigator of nature and as a philosophical thinker. FRENZEL has written an article under the title—suggested by the Edda—"Twilight of the Gods," an article which NIPPOLD pronounces "classical."

One of the very ablest replies to STRAUSS is from the pen of PHILIPPSON, the representative of reformatory Judaism, widely known by his numerous vigorous and brilliant works. HAUSRATH has written on the New Testament history. SPÖRRI is of the school of "liberal Protestant" theology. JÜRGEN BONA MEYER is Professor of Philosophy at Bonn.

The latest works from German hands which have reached us are FROHSCHAMMER'S "The

New Science and the New Faith," ZIEGLER'S "Reply to Huber," and STUTZ's Work (1874).

In America, the discussion has been opened by reviews in the April number of the "Methodist Quarterly," and of the "Presbyterian Quarterly." The latter article is by PROF. HENRY B. SMITH. He designs to follow it by a further discussion, but as it stands, it establishes a claim to a place among the best things which the theme has called forth.

Holland is very strongly represented in RAUWENHOFF and SCHOLTEN, professors at Leyden, two of the ablest writers of our day. VERA, of Naples, has reviewed STRAUSS at great length, from the Hegelian point of view, of which STRAUSS was originally an ardent supporter, and which, indeed, furnishes the basis for his critical works. MARIANO has reviewed (Rome, 1874) both STRAUSS and VERA.

In England STERLING has reviewed STRAUSS in the "Athenæum," June, 1873. An article by SCHOLTEN appears in "The Theological Review," May, 1873.

NIPPOLD has given an account of the literature called forth by the controversy, but even his appendix, dated August 11th, 1873, was too early to foreclose the bibliography of the subject.

POINTS OF INTEREST IN THE REVIEWS OF STRAUSS.

Among the many points of interest in these reviews, one of the most striking is the estimates, general and particular, which they put upon STRAUSS. They nearly without exception show that no antecedent aversion is the cause of their dislike of this book, but that on the contrary they were disposed to honor and magnify him.

"The overwhelming impression made by the "book is due to the undeniable talent of the "author, to the actual beauty of portions of it, "especially of the tributes to the great poets "and musicians of Germany, and to the nov- "elty of the idea of bringing into unity the re- "sults of theological criticism and of the latest "investigations of nature, and of welding them "together in a systematic view of the world and "of life."* "That in the darling controversy "of the hour this book has attracted almost "more notice than all the others together, is a "clear proof that STRAUSS represents one of the "great powers in the realms of mind."† "The "first question which the book forced upon us "was, how so acute a thinker, so practiced a

---

* Rauwenhoff. † Nippold.

"writer, so finished and cautious a critic, could
"lower himself to the position of a blindly
"credulous train-bearer of the most vulgar Ma-
"terialism; at a time, too, when this view is
"beginning to decline, when even the more
"acute physiologists, in the most explicit terms
"and with a full statement of their reasons, are
"abandoning the materialistic explanation of
"the phenomena of mind. The solution is
"found in the fact that STRAUSS is and remains
"a combatant in the sphere of theology, and
"seeks subsidiary troops from every direction
"to sustain him there."* BEYSCHLAG, PHILIPP-
SON, FRENZEL, and others pay tribute to the
personal honorableness of STRAUSS, but other
critics, as W. LANG, point to special instances
of unfair dealing in his book. "Of construct-
"ive reason he shows but a feeble trace; of the
"heart, in what it truly holds, and of its meas-
"ureless importance for the race, he seems to
"have not a glimpse. In the scientific part of
"his book he keeps house entirely with what
"he borrows, all his creative power and origi-
"nality deserts him, and if he were the critic of
" the book, instead of being its author, he would
"be the first to expose its weaknesses. When

---

* I. H. Fichte.

"we get out of the woods of the criticism of
"Christianity, and down into the field of re-
"ligion at large, we see STRAUSS at once desti-
"tute of resources of his own, and going into
"consultation with HUME, EPICTETUS, and LUD-
"WIG FEUERBACH. We frankly confess our
"opinion that for a German thinker he employs
"such clumsy weapons that he must himself
"feel ashamed of them. On what a feeble pub-
"lic he must have counted. He will not terrify
"us with his epithet 'old-fashioned.' His own
"imaginary counter-proofs have already become
"old-fashioned. STRAUSS calls his views 'new.'
"They are not new, they are merely the newest
"manifestation of a very ancient tendency of the
"mind. They are old, and have long been
"passed by. In vain does he cling to KANT;
"VOLTAIRE and KARL VOGT have grasped him,
"and drag him after them; vain is his fright at
"SCHOPENHAUER and VON HARTMAN; that he
"does not yield himself to them is to be put to
"the score of his weakness."*

"That a deaf man should not undertake to
"write the history of music, that a blind man
"should not propose to give the world a history
"of art, would not be disputed, and yet there be

---

* Philippson.

"curious people who think it just the thing that
"conscious, unblushing, systematic irreligious-
"ness should write the life of Jesus. Is it pos-
"sible for a man to write the history of a move-
"ment of the soul, with which he feels no con-
"geniality, but toward which he takes a purely
"negative attitude? Can a man who regards
"religion as the fantastic product of the addled
"mind, even form a judgment whether the
"history of a founder of a religion is a thing
"that could possibly be written?"*

Strauss's comparison of what claims to be Christianity in the present with the Christianity of the past, leads Dove to say: "We may in-
"deed be drawn in this way to deny with
"Strauss the claim of the present to the Chris-
"tian name, or we may, with Feuerbach, de-
"ride it as a 'dissolute, characterless, comfort-
"'able, belles-lettres, coquettish, epicurean
"'Christianity.' But is this a historic way of
"treating the matter? Would it not be just
"as fair to assume as the classic standard of
"the Germanic, the German character at a par-
"ticular period, say, for example, the time of
"Otto the Great, and allow us Germans of to-
"day to pass, at the very highest, for nothing

---

* Hausrath.

"better than 'dissolute, characterless, comfort-
"'able, belles-lettres, coquettish, epicurean Ger-
"'mans?'"

That so many of STRAUSS's old admirers should take up arms against him, is explained in some measure by the fact that his candid statement of the logical finality of his movement has been very alarming to a large class of them. The answer of this class to the question, " Are we Christians still?" has constantly been that they are Christians of the purest and the best. They do not receive Christ in his personal claims; they acknowledge in him nothing superhuman; they repudiate alike the miracles wrought by him, and the miraculous events which are parts of his own history, but all the more in the power of the etherealized, unembarrassed residuum, can they soar as Christians. They repudiate a religion *about* Christ and confine themselves to the religion *of* Christ; they, in a word, claim to be of the same religion with Christ; he is at best a mere *primus inter pares*. And yet he is hardly that—beyond the credulous adherents of the old faith, they are veritable Christians, because they have improved upon the Teacher, and are more Christian than Christ himself. But STRAUSS abandons them in this claim, and insists that it is dishonorable for himself and those who stand with him in his criticisms of Christ and Christianity, to call themselves Christians. He shows that Christianity in its very essence involves the personal claims of Christ; that to take the name of the dimly seen enthusiast of Galilee, and yet deny the miracles, without the claims of which for him, that name would never have reached us, is absurd. Jesus might have been all of truest and best that the strongest claim for him has ever asserted, "and yet," says STRAUSS, "his "doctrines would have been like leaves driven "and scattered before the wind, had not a "fond faith in his resurrection bound together "these leaves in one compact mass."* STRAUSS says, in effect, We have outgrown our old position. From knowing little of Jesus, we have advanced till we know nothing; to pretend to know anything carries us back to the old orthodox position which claims to know everything. The logic of the blind old faith is with the Creeds of the churches, the logic of the new faith is Materialism and Atheism.

STRAUSS who commenced by killing the old school of Rationalists with his myths, ends with killing the whole brood of the mythical Chris-

---

* Alt. u. Neu. Glaub. Sechst. Aufl., 73.

tians with his "new faith." The fine line he once drew between the permanent and transient in Christianity has vanished. He has got the whole in one neck now, and the blow falls. Everything in Christianity is transient. The insatiate old critic, born as he claims, to be a ruthless destroyer, having disposed of everything else, eats his own words, and Saturn-like ends the scene by devouring his own offspring. The weeping and protestations of these hapless children are the attestations of their reluctance to vanish within the expanding jaws of this tremendous old anthropophagite.

That STRAUSS greatly miscalculated the power of his leadership in this new movement is certain. "The 'We,'" says FRENZEL, "furnish, I
" fear, the matter of the philosopher's first decep-
" tion. Certainly a large number of cultivated
" persons, and these form the only class brought
" into account here, will follow his first steps; but
" with every step of his advance, the number of
" his adherents, or, rather we should style them,
" those who share his views, more and more
" melts away. Some of them will hold fast to this
" point, others to that, in the old faith. There
" are those who will not abandon the immortality
" of the soul in some shape; others will not find
" the Darwino-Vogto-Straussian primal ape at

"all to their taste. When STRAUSS reaches the
"goal of his views of religion, his view of the
"universe, he will find very few with him, and
"when out of theory he springs into the prac-
"tical, making his leap from religion into poli-
"tics, he will find himself alone." "Philoso-
"phy equally with religion, rests at last on the
"unfathomable. No man hath seen the aveng-
"ing God of the Old Testament, or God the
"Father, revealed in the New. But neither
"has any man ever taken a survey of STRAUSS's
"universe. The one equally with the other is a
"conception. ADAM the first man lives only in
"the Mosaic record, but does, perchance, DAR-
"WIN's primal ape have a better hold on life?
"He too has vanished and left no trace. The
"theologians are enthusiasts for Adam, the
"zoologists are enthusiasts for the ape. That is
"the total difference.

"If STRAUSS imagines that he is actually able,
"as he wishes, to establish his new faith and
"suppress Christianity, he seems to have fallen
"into a fatal illusion—the illusion of VOLTAIRE
"and DIDEROT. They imagined that because
"they were unbelievers themselves, the time
"must come when nobody would believe, the
"time when all men would be philosophers.
"Nevertheless with the whole development of

"humanity lying before us, we see a vanishing
"minority in the path of philosophy, an over-
"whelming majority following after religion.
"For whole ages together philosophy has been
"dumb; in no age has the voice of religion been
"silenced."

STRAUSS is charged by a number of the reviewers with ignorance, or persistent ignoring of what is strongest in opposition to his own views. He and his school are blamed with appealing to authority as arbitrarily as the most implicit orthodoxy does. VOGT and MOLESCHOTT are exalted to the place of Church Fathers. FROHSCHAMMER, after commending STRAUSS's early labors, goes on to say: "The more do we re-
"gret that STRAUSS has now gone to the op-
"posite extreme. He has forsaken the purely
"human, rational, and ideal position for which
"he battled against the supernatural and irra-
"tional position of Faith, and has fallen into
"a subhuman, materialistic theory, as ground-
"less and pernicious as the one he rejected.
"Yet to supply the defects of this very theory,
"he puts forth by way of enactment his own
"strength of faith, that sort of faith which he
"has so critically and decidedly refused to allow
"for the benefit of anything else.

"Our regret is the greater and more just,

"since we are threatened with the formation of
"a new priestcraft, a priestcraft of Atheism and
"Materialism, which will be no less fanatical
"against those who cannot accept it than 'Su-
"pernaturalism' has been; which will demand
"just as blind a faith even for its utterly ground-
"less assertions as this has done, and will
"throughout proceed in just as uncritical a
"way. Any one acquainted with the writings
"of the most renowned representatives of Ma-
"terialism, will readily perceive the truth of
"this statement. He will not fail to observe
"that this tendency shows a common affinity
"and a parallelism with that old credulous
"Supernaturalism, in the ignorant supercil-
"iousness and blind depreciation it displays
"toward philosophy, and in its disposition to
"treat all that is ideal in feeling and judgment
"as useless 'drivel' or empty fancy."

STRAUSS is censured for doing violence to his national affinities, which ought to have been with men like FICHTE the younger, WEISSE, LOTZE, and the German philosophers in general. He has renounced them all in favor of the wisdom of the French Encyclopedists, and of the "Système de la Nature." "God and "the Universe," says CARRIÈRE, "are not "merely 'two equivalents for the same thing,'

"and the total result of the entire modern
"philosophy in regard to the nature of God,
"does not end in this, as STRAUSS assures us it
"does. BAADER, SCHELLING, KRAUSE, taught
"the personality of God. LOTZE, LAZARUS, of
"the school of HERBART, WEISSE, and FICHTE
"the younger, coming rather from the direction
"of HEGEL, TRENDLENBURG, ULRICI, WIRTH,
"RITTER, HUBER, and very many other thinkers,
"have devoted comprehensive works to the
"establishment of a specific apprehension of
"this question very different from that which
"STRAUSS represents. Though STRAUSS will not
"look at these books, they are none the less
"there." CARRIÈRE specially mentions ULRICI'S
"God and Nature," as a book to which STRAUSS
ought to have had regard.

STRAUSS'S INCONSISTENCY WITH HIS EARLIER POSITION.

That STRAUSS has departed from his earlier position is acknowledged by all his reviewers. The one set charges it on him as the change of an inconsistent man. The other, which includes his most determined friends and his extremest foes, unites in declaring that his present position is but the change of ripening and of more matured consistency. STRAUSS had said: "Where shall we find in such beauty as we find "it in Jesus, that mirroring purity of soul, which "the fury of the storm may agitate but cannot "cloud? Where has there been so grand an "idea, so restless an activity, so exalted a sacri- "fice for it as in Jesus? Who has been the "founder of a work which has endowed with "as rich treasures, in as high a degree, the "masses of men and nations through the long "ages, as the work which bears the name of "Christ? As little as mankind can be without "religion, so little can they be without Christ. ". . . And this Christ, as inseparable from the "supremest shaping of religion, is historical "not mythical; he is an individual, not a bare "symbol."

From the STRAUSS of 1839, the transition is so great to the STRAUSS of 1872, that his English translator (apparently a novice, furnished with a very imperfect dictionary), has not dared fairly to reproduce all of his coarseness, in connection with the name of Christ. If STRAUSS knew how to develop legitimately from the point he abandoned to the point he has reached, the logic is resistless that there is no consistent position between the Christ of the old faith and the Materialistic Atheism of the new. But if the STRAUSS of the inferences be illogical, how shall we regard the STRAUSS of the premises?

THE GREAT PHYSICISTS.

The nature of the theme and of the time has led to a large summoning into court of the men of the past, and still more of the present, whose names add lustre to the physical sciences. Among the dead, the names most frequently cited are those of ARISTOTLE, NEWTON, KANT, LA PLACE, REIMARUS, LAMARCK, CUVIER, OKEN, LIEBIG, JOHANNES MÜLLER, EISENLOHR and RUDOLF WAGNER. HUMBOLDT'S remark, made the more telling by his general admiration of STRAUSS, is quoted: "What has not pleased me "in STRAUSS, is the levity he displays in the "sphere of natural history, in his readiness to "find the origination of the organic out of the "inorganic, and the formation of man himself "out of the primeval slime of Chaldea." AGASSIZ's influence does not seem to have been impaired even by BÜCHNER's intolerable impudence in asserting that his anti-Darwinian views were an accommodation to the Puritan atmosphere which surrounded him in America. Among the names of living authors we may mention a few which are specially prominent.

Von Baer, of Königsberg, is distinguished in the History of Development and in Zootomy. Clausius, of Bonn, is renowned as a physicist, especially in the establishment of the doctrine of heat as a mode of motion. For his merits in this he received the great Huygen's gold medal in 1870. Donders, of Utrecht, is illustrious as a physiologist and oculist, and is the founder of a great system of ophthalmology. He is "an investigator of acknowledged geni-"ality, thoroughness and many-sidedness. His "very numerous writings are distinguished by "clearness and elegance." He was the first to apply the principle of the conservation of force to the animal organism. Du Bois-Reymond, of Berlin, pupil of Johannes Müller, holds the chair of his master. His renown is very great in the general field of natural sciences, but is pre-eminently so in "animal electricity." Helmholtz, of Berlin, occupies a high position among the German physicists, and he owes his distinction in no small measure to the philosophical spirit of his investigations. He has united the most complete, many-sided, and thorough elaboration of the individual minutiæ with a range of view which takes in the whole in its greatness. By physiological investigations he has been carried to results which, at many points, touch those which **Kant** reached by purely metaphysical processes. **Lotze**, of Göttingen, is one of the most modest, and yet one of the profoundest and most brilliant of that grandest school of thinkers who are great both in physical science and in metaphysics. His "Mikrokosmus" is a classic masterpiece in both, hardly equalled, never surpassed, by any work on its theme. It required a ripe man in a ripe age to produce it. **Fechner**, of Leipzig, also distinguished in the two departments, occupies a Spinozistic-Kantian position. **Virchow** is one of the glories of the medical faculty of the University of Berlin, first President of the German Anthropological Association, and founder of Cellular Pathology.

The names of **Wundt**, **Czolbe**, **Planck**, **Häckel**, **Schleiden**, **Carus**, **Snell**, **Vierordt**, **Tyndall**, **Barnard** (of Columbia College, New York), **Bronn**, **Kölliker**, **Nägele** are also among those cited in the controversy. The array is an imposing one, and its main weight is thrown against Materialism, and with increasing unity and force. Science is already fulfilling the grand duty which **Scholten** says is imposed on her, the duty of repelling the assertion that "science is materialistic." "No possible "explanation," says **Barnard**, "of mental phe-

"nomena can be founded upon a hypothesis which attempts to identify them with physical forces.... The organic world furnishes just as conclusive evidence of the existence of an influence superior to force, as the physical world exhibits of the existence of force itself.... As physicists, we have nothing to do with mental philosophy. In endeavoring to reduce the phenomena of mind under the laws of matter we wander beyond our depth, we establish nothing certain, we bring ridicule upon the name of positive science, and achieve but a single undeniable result, that of unsettling in the minds of multitudes, convictions which form the basis of their chief happiness. ... There is certainly a field which it is not the province of physical science to explore, and which, if we are wise, we shall carefully refrain from invading."

"I am no materialist," says Huxley, "but, on the contrary, believe Materialism to involve grave philosophical error.... In so far as my study of what specially characterizes the Positive Philosophy has led me, I find therein little or nothing of any scientific value, and a great deal which is as thoroughly antagonistic to the very essence of science as anything in ultramontane Catholicism.... The further sci-

"ence advances, the more extensively and con-
"sistently will all the phenomena of nature be
"represented by materialistic formulæ and sym-
"bols. But the man of science who, forgetting
"the limits of philosophical inquiry, slides from
"these formulæ and symbols into what is com-
"monly understood by Materialism, seems to
"me to place himself on a level with the mathe-
"matician who should mistake the x's and y's,
"with which he works his problems, for real
"entities, and with this further disadvantage,
"as compared with the mathematician, that the
"blunders of the latter are of no practical con-
"sequence, while the errors of systematic Ma-
"terialism may paralyze the energies and de-
"stroy the beauty of a life."

"The passage from the physics of the brain
"to the corresponding facts of consciousness,"
says TYNDALL, "is unthinkable. . . . On both
"sides of the zone here assigned to the materi-
"alist he is equally helpless. . . . When we
"endeavor to pass . . . from the phenomena
"of physics to those of thought, we meet a
"problem which transcends any conceivable
"expansion of the powers which we now pos-
"sess. We may think over the subject again
"and again, but it eludes all intellectual pre-
"sentation. We stand at length face to face

"with the Incomprehensible. The territory of
"physics is wide, but it has its limits, from
"which we look with vacant gaze into the re-
"gion beyond... Having exhausted physics, and
"reached its very rim, the real mystery still
"looms beyond us. We have, in fact, made
"no step toward its solution. And thus will
"it ever loom, ever beyond the bound of knowl-
"edge."

From these utterances, which are parallel with those given by ULRICI, from DONDERS, and DU BÖIS-REYMOND, and which could be multiplied indefinitely, it is very clear that gross injustice may be done to men of science, by confounding their Materialism and Non-theism, *in the sphere of physical science*, with a total Materialism and Atheism in a different sphere. For the physicist, *as such*, is occupied wholly with the question, What does physics prove? and not at all with the question, What do other sources of knowledge prove? He knows that unproven is not disproven, and that unproven by one still less means disproven by all. That sort of folly is for the blatant novice who would rather talk " big," than talk wisely. The Materialist in matter is not of necessity a Materialist in mind, and a non-theist in the law may be a hearty theist before the law. Physical science, can as such, be neither theistic nor atheistic, for physical science is totally occupied with second causes, and theism and atheism are alike occupied with the question of final cause. That is a question not of physics but of metaphysics. Physics can accumulate the rich stores of material, to which both theist and atheist may resort, but in its exclusive sphere it is neither to be lauded for the uses made of them by the one, nor condemned for the abuses of them made by the other. A Natural Theology now could be made grander than any that has ever been written. If the scientist claims the common right to use the materials of physics for speculative purposes, we have to grant it. If in doing it, he shows that while in the sphere of physics he may be strong, in that of metaphysics he is weak, we must not condemn him as the strong physicist but as the weak metaphysician. It is not science but the want of science which is at fault. When physical science, the science of phenomena and of second causes, not of essence and ultimate cause, reaches any point, at which the next step involves either affirmation or denial of a Supreme Cause, it has reached its Rubicon. Every step after that is in defiance of its own commission, an assumption of authority that does not belong to it. It is Imperator on its own side, it is Usurper on the other. Physical science may give us Chemistries, Geologies, Treatises on Mechanics, but it has no right to give us manuals of Ethics, or systems of Philosophy or of Theology, though the writers of manuals and systems may find rich suggestions in it for both.

Much is said in these reviews of the mischievous spirit and tendency of Strauss's book in various aspects, social, political, and religious. "We had not reckoned it possible," says Rauwenhoff, "that David Friedrich Strauss "should offer himself as the mouthpiece of a "reactionary conservatism like that of Prussia. "It is a new illustration of the way in which "Skepticism invariably ends in bringing grist "to the mill of Absolutism. . . . Strauss comes "involuntarily to the deification of the strong "arm. His tranquillity in view of the future of "the German race, rests on his trust in the mil- "itary despotism of Prussia. Goethe and Hum- "boldt, the heroes of culture and advance, are "dead, but, thank Heaven, we have in their "place Bismarck and Moltke, the heroes of "diplomacy and war! . . . This is a time to "press the claim of freedom over against that "of statutory regulation, the claim of right "over against might, of culture over against mil-

"itary despotism. And at this crisis comes this
"son of Swabia, this independent man of science,
"this standard-bearer of free thinking—comes
"with a new programme for state and society,
"and in this programme he speaks for sound
"popular improvement, for freedom of the
"press, for elementary and higher education,
"for the moral exaltation of the spirit of the
"people—not a solitary word; but in place of
"all these we have a commendation of the old
"state-policy, under the broad shield of Bis-
"marck, with the sword of the Empire in his
"hand, and in the background, as the head-
"stone of this edifice of state, the scaffold. . . .
"What good might he have wrought had he
"employed his power as a writer to cast into
"the wakened national feeling seeds of the
"spirit of freedom, of humanity, of civic virtue,
"of progress in trade and the industrial pur-
"suits, in science and art; had he said to his
"people that as they had once more risen to
"the first rank among European powers they
"had new duties to fulfil, that Germany was to
"show to the world how a great people can wed
"Freedom to Order, can become the bulwark
"of the Right, and go forth upon the pathway
"of a true progress. He might have taught
"them this. What has he taught them? I see

"but one possible practical application which
"Germans can make of STRAUSS's book, and
"that is to run away from the Church as fast as
"they can, and find safety from all sorts of
"perils by creeping under the skirts of the
"Chancellor of the Empire.

"STRAUSS may be a fine thinker, but he has no
"heart for *his own* people. No! and more than
"this, he has no heart for *the people* at all. He
"asks, 'Is LESSING's "Nathan" or GOETHE's
"'"Hermann and Dorothea" harder to under-
"'stand or less replete with the "truths of sal-
"'vation," or does it embrace fewer golden sen-
"'tences than an Epistle of Paul or one of John's
"'Discourses of Christ?' Is this sport or ear-
"nest? When the poor man out of the masses
"must put away his Bible, and asks for some-
"thing from which he can draw a word to build
"up his soul, we are to put in his hands 'Nathan
"the Wise' and 'Hermann and Dorothea.'
"STRAUSS himself could not have the heart to
"practice what he recommends. Even he must
"have a suspicion at least, what this Bible, on
"which he charges so many offences, means to
"the simple, pious soul. Understand it! Alas!
"spare yourself the trouble of explaining it if
"you imagine that your explanation is for the
"first time to unseal the springs of power in life,

"and of courage in death, which this old Scrip-
"ture word has for the pious poor. You feel
"an intellectual pride in deciphering the num-
"ber of the Beast in the Apocalypse; but think
"you that the simple Bible-reader has been
"waiting for your discovery, to dispel the ter-
"rors of death, in the light of that heavenly Je-
"rusalem, where God himself shall wipe away
"all tears from his eyes? You may explain the
"train of the connection in the Epistle to the
"Romans better than LUTHER could, but with
"the words 'the righteous shall live by his
"faith,' LUTHER broke from the neck of his
"native land the yoke of superstition. You
"speak of the classics? Here, too, we have
"classics, these old Psalmists of Israel, whose
"sacred poetry, though two thousand years
"have past, wakens the tenderest chords of the
"human heart. And Jesus—Jesus, whom you
"call a visionary, a laggard in the development
"of mind—is he who spake the words, every
"one of which is felt in the incalculable sum
"of blessings imparted to our race in all its
"struggles and sorrows... The people is indeed
"uncultivated, but in some things it has sound
"feeling, and it would rise in wrath at the at-
"tempt to substitute, on the wall of the poor
"cottage room, the head of GOETHE for the Head

"crowned with thorns, or to put the three well
"selected, well arranged quartettes in place of
"the old hymns in the Church, sung to the sol-
"emn cadence of the organ. To attempt it
"would bring proof that it is one thing to play
"the trifler with the old faith, and another and
"a wholly different one to dislodge it from the
"hearts and lives of the people.

"Had STRAUSS seen much of the life of the
"people, it is impossible that there should have
"been no note of sadness at the close of his
"book, in the contemplation of the loss involved
"to mankind, were his faith really to supplant
"the old faith. He could not speak so light-
"heartedly of man's sense of imperfection, . . of
"the abandoning of trust in providence, . . of the
"unsatisfying in life. Could I believe as STRAUSS
"believes, I might feel myself bound to utter
"my convictions, but I think I could not refrain
"from tears as I spoke. I should weep at the
"thought that there were thousands who would
"not merely lose what I lost, but who in this
"loss would see everything vanish, all that
"touched their life with a brighter hue, all that
"imparted to its sordidness something of poetry,
"to its sadness something of consolation.

"No man can see unmoved, the cynicism
"which tears away from a child its ideal—and

"STRAUSS! the people for whom thou hast no "more than this cynic comfort, this people is "but a child, a child of poverty and sorrow."

HUBER quotes the saying of MAZZINI that "the doctrine of Materialism is the philosophy "of all epochs which are withering to the grave, "and of all nations sinking to extinction." "We dare not allow," says HUBER, at the close of his book, "the spirit of the idealistic philos- "ophy to be lost, if we are to have any guaran- "tee of a great and happy future for our native "land."

THE POLITICAL ELEMENTS IN STRAUSS.

STRAUSS has had an extraordinary felicity in disgusting men of both the great political tendencies. The Conservatives are disgusted with his destructivism of principles, and the Progressives with his heartless sycophancy to the ruling powers, in practice. He lays the foundation of a Red Republic, and builds upon it a structure of absolute Despotism. Neither party is satisfied with either part. The Red Republicans abhor the foundation, for it is made the foundation for monarchy. The Monarchists abhor the structure, for it is made to rest on the quicksands of the most ultra infidelity, which they know demoralizes the people, and gives terrible power to the dangerous classes. Each class abhors the thing they would, because it is bound up with the thing they would not.

H. Lang, "the radical of radicals, and one of Strauss's most fervent admirers," expresses the disappointment he had experienced in reading his last book. "Rarely," says he, "have my "anticipations proved so empty, as on the read-"ing of this book. To be sure it contains not "a few things which are suggestive and beau-"tifully put, but as a whole it disgusted me; "it was pervaded by such an air of senility, "an aristocratic daintiness, thrusting out of "sight the real forces of life, a sort of dis-"agreeable sourness and crabbedness, when I "looked for that repose of unprejudiced esti-"mate, which is the token of a wise man."

"Our author," says Rauwenhoff, "is a "criminalist of the old style. He laughs at all "the twaddle about humanity and the rights of "men. He huzzaed for the laws against the "Jesuits; he went in for a summary taking of "the people of the International over the "border, and he sighs at the thought how many "are likely to give the gallows the slip."

"It is worthy of note," says Michelis, "how "anxiously Strauss regards the probability of

"an outbreak of savagery in the world of the
"new faith, and how desirous he is to restore or
"preserve all the means of coercive restraint.
"The death-penalty is to be retained and made
"more general (though STRAUSS nowhere has a
"place for the element of expiation for guilt).
"The right of voting is to be restricted, the
"right of mutual association on the part of
"workingmen is to be abrogated. He is a
"friend of nobility, monarchy, war, and, as a
"matter of course, standing armies. What in-
"fatuation! As if everything of that sort would
"not bend like willow-twigs, or be torn up by
"the roots, like pines, when the hurricane
"breaks loose, which is sure to come, if the
"people should ever reach STRAUSS's convic-
"tions, and act them out in earnest."

THE REACTIONARY TENDENCY OF STRAUSS'S BOOK.

Of the tendency of the book by *reaction*, the general opinion of the reviewers is that expressed by SPÖRRI: "Anxious souls, when they
"see themselves reduced to the alternative of
"choosing between the Church-faith intact, and
"the results here offered, may be seized with
"terror at all criticism, and throw themselves
"into the arms of orthodoxy; or, taking warn-

"ing from STRAUSS, that they cannot stand fast
"by the Protestant orthodoxy, nor even by that
"of the Old Catholics, may find themselves
"guided in the straight path to Rome. Of those
"who have been standing in an attitude of indif-
"ference to the Church and to Christianity, and
"who will clap their hands, there is a large class
"with whom it will not be pleasant for STRAUSS
"to be associated. Others, thoughtful of the
"welfare of the people, will continue to com-
"mend othodoxy as the only proper diet for
"the masses, with the understanding, however,
"that they are not to be expected to partake of
"this nutriment themselves." "On many a
"reader, however, this book may have an effect
"like that which the philosophy of SCHOPEN-
"HAUER had on STRAUSS. It may produce in
"such a reader a reaction against this whole
"method of treating the Christian religion, and
"may recall to him the secret threads which
"still bind him to Christianity."

Of the provision for an effectual antidote to STRAUSS's book, RAUWENHOFF says, at the end of his discussion: "STRAUSS's style of thinking
"is a power which is not to be vanquished by
"anathemas, or by critical processes. The sole
"power before which it must give way is the
"power of a religion, which, without impairing

"in any respect the just claims of science, and
"without bringing any derangement into the
"natural unfolding of social life, shall permeate
"every part of our human existence with its
"sanctifying and quickening might."

ULRICI'S REVIEW OF STRAUSS.

Distinguished among the numerous reviews of STRAUSS is the Criticism contributed by ULRICI to the "Zeitschrift für Philosophie und Philosophische Kritik."

DR. HERMANN ULRICI (born 1806), Professor of Philosophy in the University of Halle, is known to English readers by the translation of his work on the Dramatic Art of Shakspeare, London, 1846. He has written other works on Literary History and Criticism; but the great strength of his life has been put into works of which the English public knows little, but of which it would be a great gain to it to know much. To all students of the best philosophical writings of living German authors, ULRICI is known as the author of a number of works which show a rare mastery of the physical and metaphysical sciences; works which are models of logical thinking and of noble style. He is not an ambitious novice, pulling himself into notice by dragging at the skirts of a celebrity of the hour; but is a man who, in the best elements of true renown, is STRAUSS's superior.

ULRICI is not a theologian, and does not write from a theological point of view. For the immediate moral force and effectiveness of the review we translate, this is an advantage. It anticipates the very pitiful but very common pretence, by which the school of loose thinkers conveniently sets aside a work from the hand of one whose life business it is to defend the great principles of a pure Theism. They solve his defence by insisting that he makes it only because it is his business. The very men who under the pretence of physical theory, are little more than uncalled dabblers in theology, of whose primary principles they show themselves too ignorant even to misrepresent them effectively, make an outcry against the theologian as an intruder into other men's province—*their* province—when, however modestly and ably, he defends revealed truth against pseudo-scientific assumption. In ULRICI we have a great philosophical thinker, deciding by the processes of a sober, logical philosophy the claim which STRAUSS was most ambitious to establish for himself, the claim to be a rational thinker. It is a claim with the fall of which his book falls.

The confutation of STRAUSS's philosophy is the completest confutation of what is most important in his "new faith." If in this he is not a philosophical thinker, he is nothing. In the album of the Crown Princess of Prussia, the year before his death (he died February 9th, 1874), STRAUSS wrote: "Though the wise and "honored refuse me a place among them, I "shall not complain, if I be but reckoned with "the *rational.*" Whatever be the place of STRAUSS in the judgment of after generations, it will surely not be with "the rational," if the rational are those who have used the highest reason in the service of the purest truth.

ULRICI's review shows his characteristic ability. It is a masterpiece of logic, fact, and practical force. It is clear and cogent, compact yet comprehensive. Letting STRAUSS speak for himself, both in statement and argument, it meets him calmly and answers him overwhelmingly. STRAUSS is fond of the weapons of ridicule, but he is no master in the use of them, but he provokes sarcasm in reply, less by his feeble, and sometimes coarse wit, than by his ineffable, self-satisfied absurdity. In his worst displays of this sort he cannot be burlesqued, he can only be exhibited. ULRICI's review never *makes* STRAUSS ridiculous; that it *shows* him so, is STRAUSS's own fault.

Every one desires to know what STRAUSS held and why he held it, but very many have not the time or the inclination to read his book. Every one should wish to know how STRAUSS is overthrown on the very ground he has selected for his battle. Few, however, have access to the ampler works which have been written in reply to him, and few would have time or desire to read them, if they had. As warfare grows older, battles become shorter. In modern tactics the demonstrated ability to do a thing often makes it unnecessary to do it. To pierce the centre makes the beating of the wings a mere matter of detail, and in ULRICI's review STRAUSS's centre is annihilated. His wings are not worth saving, and not worth beating.

This volume, then, is enough for its end. It is a discussion, scientific, yet perfectly intelligible to every educated reader, of all the most vital of the speculative questions of the day. It furnishes one of the best antidotes to the widely circulated and dangerous book of STRAUSS, the weaknesses and internal contradictions of which it lays bare. To the general reader, as well as to the man of science, to all who are in the perils or doubts of Materialism,

Ulrici's "Review of Strauss," rich in matter and classic in execution, yet small in bulk, will be invaluable. It shows how necessary and great a part is borne by true philosophical thinking in the confutation of the false. If Germany gives to the world the ablest presentations of the wrong, she also furnishes the noblest vindications of the right.

Fichte says of Ulrici's review, "With such "keenness of logic, such inexorable sequence of "conclusion, has it laid bare the internal con- "tradictions, the hastiness of inference, the un- "sustained assumption, which reveal themselves "in the particular parts as well as in the gen- "eral position of Strauss's book, as to place be- "yond all doubt the final judgment in regard to "its *philosophical* value." Nippold says: "To "consider it necessary to say a single word in "regard to Ulrici's significance in the devel- "opment of the modern philosophy, would be "as absurd as the attempt to ignore a Lotze or "a Trendlenburg. His judgment on Strauss, "as a philosophical thinker, cuts with an al- "most unsurpassable acuteness." "Any one "who will recall," says another German re- viewer, "the haughty self-sufficiency with which "Strauss has been making his appeal to 'phi- "losophy,' meaning the Hegelian, as if there "were no other, and pleasing himself with the "idea of being a philosopher, will readily un-"derstand, why among all the writings in oppo-"sition to his book, that of Ulrici must most "deeply cut to the quick his gigantic vanity."

In the translation, Ulrici's notes have been incorporated into the text, but are distinguished by square brackets. The various subdivisions of his discussion have been numbered and furnished with headings. All his citations of Strauss have been carefully verified. Where Strauss has made a change in the later editions, the change is noted, and the paging of the sixth edition is added to that of the edition used by Ulrici. The Introduction has been designed to give a general view of the Materialism of our day, and a special presentation of the most important points in the controversy raised by the book of Strauss. Many of the strongest and most brilliant things which have been called forth in the reviews of Strauss are brought together, and, with Ulrici's critique, will help to make the volume an epitome of the great points in discussion. It will aid the reader who desires to be brought fully abreast with the results and questions of the latest investigation and speculation of our day.

ULRICI'S REVIEW OF STRAUSS:

"THE OLD FAITH AND THE NEW FAITH."

I.

STRAUSS CONSIDERED AS A PHILOSOPHICAL THINKER.

DAVID FRIEDRICH STRAUSS is a celebrity. All his works have run through so and so many editions. The most important of them belong to the department of Theology, or, to speak more accurately, to the department of the Philosophy of Religion. It is a matter of interest, therefore, even to the philosopher by profession, when a man like STRAUSS comes forth in the evening of his life with a confession of his faith. Our interest, however, in this direction is, as a matter of course, confined to the question, What are the philosophical grounds—what is the philosophical tenableness of this new faith? The question whether STRAUSS is right or wrong, or how far he may be right or wrong, in his way of apprehending the origin, development, significance, truth or untruth of historical Christianity, and of the doctrines of the Church, is a question of a purely theological character, with which we have here nothing to do. We are interested *solely* in STRAUSS as *a philosophical thinker*. We have read his book, simply because we felt warranted in the assumption, that a philosopher who had reached the distinguished position held by STRAUSS among scientific writers, would mean by the faith to which he gives his adherence something more than his mere *individual* faith, his *subjective* view or conviction. Such a faith could inspire very little interest in our mind. We assumed that this new faith would be offered and argued, philosophically, as a form and apprehension of religion objectively justified. In this expectation we have been grievously disappointed. We find, on the contrary, that the "new faith" is utterly destitute of any philosophical foundation. In fact we are forced to the conviction, that the book before us very closely resembles a philosophical bankrupt's statement on the part of its renowned author.

This conviction of ours, which to the mass of the admirers of STRAUSS and of the disciples of the new faith, may seem supremely paradoxical, and supremely heretical, we have made it our task thoroughly to vindicate, and we are not without hope of being able to do it.

We lay down as a rule or criterion the principle, that a philosopher, who on essential points not only puts forth as established truths assertions which are completely without evidence, and wholly untenable, but contradicts himself again and again, has no claim to be called a philosopher. The validity of the principle will be granted by *every* philosopher, and, it is to be hoped, by all who claim to be a part of what is called the cultivated class.

II.

WHAT STRAUSS PROPOSES IN "THE NEW FAITH AND THE OLD FAITH:" HIS REAL AIM THE DESTRUCTION OF THE OLD FAITH.

At an early stage of the discussion STRAUSS explains what he means, and what he does not mean by the "we," in whose name he speaks. "We do not involve in our plan any changes at "all, for the time, in the outside world. We "do not dream of overthrowing any of the "churches, for we know that to innumerable "persons a church is still a necessity. It does "not seem to us that the time has yet come even "for a new construction—not the construction "of a church, but, after the church has crum- "bled into final ruin, the construction of a new

"organization of the ideal elements in the vari-
"ous forms of national life. Nor would we
"merely patch and vamp up the old structures,
"for in such a course we see only a repression
"of the process of formation. We can only
"work in stillness, so that in the future some-
"thing new may shape itself out of that disin-
"tegration of the old, which must inevitably
"come."*

This means, then, that STRAUSS has taken up his pen not for the new organization of the ideal elements in the life of nations—for the time has not come for that—but only for the future self-evolution of something new, out of the inevitable disintegration of the old. But this "new," if it involve faith and religion, can consist only in a new formation of the "ideal elements in the forms of national life," and these are the only things on which it is possible to work, if we are to organize them anew. In the sphere of the ideal, organization is but a substitute, a more pregnant word for formation; and not in the future, but in the present only can we work *for* the future. This is a problem then for whose solution the time has not come, for whose solution, therefore, it is *impossible* to work, and

---

* Der Alt. u. Neu. Glaub. Sechst. Aufl. 1873, p. 8.

this is the solution on which STRAUSS goes to work. This work he proposes to do "in *stillness;*" and to accomplish this end, he publishes books, which he no doubt expects and wishes may find a hearty response.

The "new," which he has in his eye, is something which is to form "*itself of itself*," but he is going to "work" so that it may form itself. He proposes then to work for something which has no need of his co-working, and which can be advantaged by his work, either not at all, or only so far as his work prepares the ground by relieving it of rubbish and levelling it—in a word, by a complete removal of the old. But this, it seems, is not the purpose of his work, for he "does not dream of overthrowing any of the churches." But as in this declaratory act one statement is all the time contradicting another, we are, at the very outstart, left standing in hopeless perplexity before the question: What is STRAUSS really aiming at? What was his precise object in writing and publishing his book?

In the course of his discussion, indeed, we are not long left in ignorance as to what he purposes, and as to what he is doing. It is very speedily apparent, in spite of his protestation to the contrary, that he has no definite aim beyond the destruction of the old. This is rendered very clear, in part, by his elaborate assaults not only upon the orthodox apprehension of Christianity, but upon every other, even the free or rationalistic view. It is clear, also, from the fact that the new, with which he would fill up the empty space, and which he styles "The Modern View of the World," is at bottom nothing new, and nothing at all positive, but is the pure negation of faith, as it is a downright repudiation of all the "ideal elements" of our human estate—it is nothing more than naked atheism and materialism.

III.

"ARE WE STILL CHRISTIANS?"

Into that polemic, as we have already said, we do not design to enter. We commit to theologians the answer to the question, What was the teaching of Christ, can we understand it, and what is its meaning? We pass over, therefore, the entire first part of the book, bearing the superscription, "Are we still Christians?" It needs no such discussion to make it clear that this is a question, the answer to which every one will determine at his own pleasure. Whether STRAUSS does, or does not regard himself as a Christian, is in itself of no consequence at all, so far as the interests of Christianty are involved. To be sure, he declares it impossible that a cultivated man should profess the Christian religion, but that amounts to nothing, so long as the actual existence of such men furnishes the direct confutation of the asserted impossibility. It does not follow, therefore, that because "we" are no longer Christians, Christianity must "inevitably" go to the ground.

IV.

"HAVE WE RELIGION STILL?"

After responding in the negative to his own first question, STRAUSS goes on to a second one: "Have we religion still?" He introduces it with a "glance at the rise and early development of religion in the human race." As we know nothing *historically* in regard to the "rise" and "earliest" development of religion, the glance which STRAUSS casts on it is of course *philosophical*, and his opinion on the matter, to have any value at all, must be philosophically (psychologically) confirmed. In place, however, of any confirmation, and in place of all further investigation, he decides the question in advance in the sense of atheism. He asserts that "HUME is certainly justified in maintaining that

"it has not been the disinterested impulse to-
"ward the attainment of knowledge and truth,
"but the thoroughly selfish impulse toward
"well-being, which originally led men to re-
"ligion, and that the disagreeable far more
"than the pleasant has been operative as religi-
"ous motive. The Epicurean derivation of re-
"ligion from fear, has in it something indis-
"putably correct. If everything went as man
"wishes it, if he always had what he needs, did
"his plans never miscarry, and were he not
"schooled by painful experiences, to look forth
"sadly on the future, it is hardly probable that
"the idea of a superior Being (in the religious
"sense) would ever be aroused in him. He
"would have thought, it must be as it is, and
"would have accepted it in stolid indiffer-
"ence."* Thereupon he gives us quite a pretty, almost poetical picture of the life of nature as it is led by men in their earliest period, just as they spring from the bosom of nature. This is done to show us how under the influence of fear, they come to personify the powers of nature, and to make their gods out of them. With this the question in its preliminary stage is finished up. It is certainly a pity, that this

---

* Alt. u. Neu. Glaub., p. 93, Sechs. Aufl. 96.

picture, which is meant to supply the place of an argument, is nothing more than poetry, in fact is simply fiction. To this hour the child personifies the inanimate things which are around it, but not from fear. It just as freely personifies objects which it associates with friendliness and goodness, as those which seem to be enemies, and excite its fears. Everything whose effects it experiences, it regards as a living being, endowed with soul, and will, and activity. The reason of this is, that it has thus far known no other operation than a personal one, no other cause than that activity which goes forth from willing and wishing, and yet, in virtue of that law of causality, which unconsciously and involuntarily controls its thinking, it finds itself necessitated to assume that there is a cause for everything which happens to it. If it always went with man as he wishes, if he always had what he needs, if no plan miscarried, in short if, as the proverb phrases it, roasted pigeons flew into his mouth, it is quite possible that he would accept the situation "with stolid indifference," like cattle grazing in the pastures. But then under these circumstances he would probably not have been man at all, would have formed no plans, would have had no questionings touching the future, would not have troubled himself about the nature of things, the grounds and causes of events, and topics of a similar sort, but, in "stolid indifference," resigning himself to the perceptions of the senses, and the pleasures of sense, would have passed his days, like the cattle in grassy meadows. It is not then fear alone which is the immediate source of religion. With it is associated the question after the causes of phenomena, the causes of the good and evil events in nature. Rising as it does involuntarily, having its spring in the very depths of man's nature, forcing itself on him in the natural events and natural conditions of his own being, it is this question which makes man man, it is this which announces him to be man, and this question is part of the immediate source of religion. It is because he conceives of the operations, as operations or manifestations of a superior power, that he is overwhelmed with a feeling unknown to the animal, the feeling of dependence, and of conditioned being. This invests his fears and hopes with intelligent *consciousness;* by it he reaches the conception of a power reigning beyond him, and above him, revealing itself sometimes as his friend, sometimes as his foe. And as he, like the child, knows up to this period no other operation than that which is personal, proceeding from will, acting in accordance with aim and purpose, he personifies the potencies of nature, which are made known in their various activities, and not alone with fear and shrinking, but also with love and hope, regards them as superior beings. For it is an arbitrary, groundless assertion, that the earliest, the primal deities were exclusively gods of fear and terror. In all the grades of religious development, even the very lowest, we find that there were good and beneficent deities, as well as evil and inimical ones. In some instances there were *none but* good deities, in no case were there evil ones only. The mental law of causality, the notion of cause, the consciousness of dependence and limitation, demands not only the conception but the acceptance and admission of an ultimate supreme cause, a cause which is not the mere operation of another cause. This conception of the conditioned is only possible when we distinguish the conditioned from the conditioning, and the conditioning, in and of itself, purely as conditioning, is necessarily unconditioned. Hence throughout, wherever a development of religion takes place, the religious consciousness shapes itself into a faith in the existence of a supreme, unconditioned, absolute cause, which as such must be one only, must be self-determining, and must consequently be a spiritual force and activity.

V.

STRAUSS'S THEORY OF THE RISE OF RELIGION.

All we have urged has often enough been set forth in sharp, logical demonstration. STRAUSS ignores the whole of it. To him "monotheism" is the result of the "life of a horde" shut up in itself. It is in itself no witness of a higher training of the religious consciousness, but just as the case may be, it is higher or lower than the developed polytheism, of the Greeks for example. He clings so closely to his principle of fear, that he brings it even into the ethical elements of religion: "The further to "wit a people advances in civilization, the less "does it restrict its view to nature, whether in "her terrors or in her blessings, and the more "does human life, with its various relations, "come to be regarded as a momentous matter. "And in the lives of men, the larger the pro- "portion of insecurity and hazard, the greater "the dependence on circumstances, the more "unavailing human aid appears, the more co- "gently does man feel the need of assuming "powers in affinity with his own being, whom

" he can approach with his wishes and petitions.
" At this point the moral nature of man comes
" in as a co-operative factor. Man desires to be
" protected not only against the passions of
" others, but would have his own loftier striv-
" ing guarded against the powers of his own
" sensual nature, for back of the demands of
" his own conscience, he places (by way of sup-
" port) a Deity endowed with the authority to
" command."* What an amazingly odd creature man is to be sure! For the sake of his
sensual well-being, he transforms the powers of
nature into deities, who, by prayers, gifts, offer-
ings and things of the sort, are led to favor him
and to change their minds, and then he furnishes these very same deities with mandatory
power *against* his sensual appetites and selfish
will! Though the will, the arbitrary volition of
the bad man is a thoroughly internal act, which
has no reference at all to his outward natural
life, and the forces of nature which condition it,
he involves himself in this contradiction without
noticing that it is a contradiction, and that in so
doing he does nothing more than impose upon
himself! And stranger still: in this illusion,
this offspring of a terrified imagination, he has

---

* Alt. u. N. Glaub. 57, Sechst. Aufl. 100, 101.

such a firm faith, that for its sake he endures the sorest sufferings, and joyously submits to death itself, though he has invented the whole thing only for the sake of his bodily earthly well-being!

VI.

STRAUSS'S REPUDIATION OF THE ARGUMENT FOR THE EXISTENCE OF GOD.

If faith in God be no more than the contradictory result of human fear, it can, of course, furnish no proof of the existence of God. STRAUSS repeats therefore the old assertion, often enough refuted, that what is styled the cosmological proof is false, inasmuch as it leads us beyond the world to a cause distinct from it. From the fact "that every particular being in "the world has its ground in another particular "being, which is again related in the same way "to another," it does not follow, he argues, "that the totality of individual things has its "ground in one being who is not in a similar "relation, a being which, unlike the rest, has "not its ground in another, but in itself." That would be an inference, he argues, lacking all internal coherence, and destitute of all conclusiveness. Rather, "If each of the things in the

"world has its ground in another, and so on
"forever, we do not reach the conception of a
"cause whose operation would be the world,
"but of a substance whose accidents are the
"particular beings in the world: we do not
"reach a God, but a universe, resting on itself,
"abiding in its uniformity amid the eternal
"shifting of phenomena."* STRAUSS confounds
the *notion* of causality with the *mental law* of
causality. The notion of causality may allow,
at least by the aid of some plausible twistings
and turnings, of being transmuted into the notion of substantiality, and this is what STRAUSS
has done. But with the *mental law* of causality
this is simply impossible. When an operation
takes place—an event, a process, a change—that
law *compels* us to assume a cause distinct from the
effect, even where we cannot tell what the cause
is. The cause must be *distinct* from the effect,
otherwise there would be no twofoldness, there
would not be cause *and* effect, there would be
only identity, and consequently there would be
no cause. In virtue of this mental law, we cannot conceive of an endless series of causes and
effects—which is in itself a process of thinking
which is incapable of being carried out—but we

---

* P. 113, Sechst. Aufl. 116.

are *forced* to presuppose a cause, which is not in turn the mere effect of another, but which is pure, ultimate, and consequently unconditioned cause. On any other supposition we would have effects *only*, and no causes; but effect without cause is inconceivable. This purely unconditioned cause is distinguished from all things in the world, not in that "it has its ground in itself," but in the very fact that it is the cause of the world: it *has* no ground and no cause whatever, but it *is* the cause of all beside, it is the only true cause. For the law of causality does not affirm that all that *exists* must have a cause, but only that all that is *effected* or produced, all that happens, all that comes into being, must have a cause. Inasmuch as this is a universal mental law it never occurs to the unprejudiced, unsophisticated understanding to doubt its universal validity. It is only a sort of reflection ruled by a particular tendency, sophistic, and tangling itself in its self-manufactured notions and assumptions, which makes the attempt to rid itself of this law, and thus plunges itself deeper and deeper into contradictions and absurdities. This is precisely the case with STRAUSS. A universe "resting on itself" is an absurdity, for the universe does not "rest," and as a "universe" can have no basis, neither in something else—for if there were something apart from it it would be no universe—nor in itself, for a basis which bears the existent nature in itself, and is itself the nature it bears, is like the pig-tail of Baron Munchausen, by which he held himself dangling in the air. And a universe "abiding in its uniformity amid the eternal shifting of phenomena" is a contradiction in the adjective, because that which changes does not remain *uniform*, and because a changing phenomenon, which has not in it an essence which puts forth the phenomenon, and changes with it, is *no* phenomenon, but an empty illusion. This alternation, this rising and passing away of the phenomena, moreover, must have a cause, and the cause must be different from its effect. This phenomenal universe therefore—the only one we know—must have a cause distinct from itself.

In a similar style STRAUSS conducts his confutation of the teleological proof of the existence of God. He concedes indeed that the universe, or, as it is now the fashion to call it, the substance of the world, "manifests itself in an "infinite alternation of phenomena linked to-"gether not only causally, but with reference to "a common end."* But " nature herself teaches

---

* 114, Sechst. Aufl. 117.

"us that it is an erroneous assumption that
"nothing but conscious intelligence can produce
"that which shows adaptation to an end." "As
"in the case of animal instinct, for example,
"something takes place, which looks as if it
"were done in accordance with a conscious aim,
"and yet really is done without any such aim,
"so is it with the productions of nature."*
"How it comes that this illusive appearance
"arises, or that anything conformable to an aim
"takes place, and yet takes place without any
"preconceived conscious aim, is a riddle to
"which DARWIN has given a brilliant solution,
"and in so doing has, to the mind of every man
"of scientific culture, done away with all Tele-
"ology." To the authentication of this point,
however, STRAUSS does not come at once, but
prepares the way for it, by a critique of the notion of God, in the recent philosophy, by a confutation of the proofs of the immortality of the soul, and by further discussions in regard to the nature of religion. He then goes on to present a summary of the results of science with reference to the formation of the world, and the origin of life on our globe. We propose to follow him in this direction, to give his argument

---

* Sechst. Aufl. 118.

all the force he may claim for it. We shall pass by the critical portions only, regarding it as a matter of supererogation to subject to review this criticism of his, the superficiality of which no one familiar with the latest philosophy will need to have demonstrated.

VII.

IMMORTALITY OF THE SOUL.

That STRAUSS should regard faith in immortality as a superstition is a matter of course. It is only a logical necessity that the denial of God should involve the denial of the immortality of the soul. It is also involved in the nature of the case, that there are not and cannot be "evidences" of the immortality of the soul, so rigid as to make its rejection impossible. None the less does STRAUSS demand this sort of evidence. The result is that he discovers that the evidences hitherto given—the weakest of which he carefully selects, ignoring the stronger ones —have no cogency. But in doing this he is simply guilty once more of confounding distinct notions. When evidences are so rigid as to make rejection impossible, we call the result *knowledge;* and that we have, in this sense, a knowledge of the immortality of the soul, no sober philosophical thinker has ever pretended. The question here at issue is that of *faith* in immortality. Faith must indeed be able to sustain itself by good objective reasons, or it would be nothing more than a subjective opinion, or a superstition. But there are reasons sufficient to justify it which are nevertheless not coercive evidences, because doubts and exceptions may be urged against them, the weight of which depends upon the subjectivity of the individual, into the balance of which they are cast. Only on this account is it faith, not knowledge. Such reasons there are, and they stand fast, despite STRAUSS's confutation; some of them in fact he has not touched at all. [That STRAUSS should make no reference to the arguments for the immortality of the soul which I have grouped together in my book, "God and Nature,"* is nothing more than was to be expected. The renowned critic confines himself, as a matter of course, to the renowned old philosophers.]

VIII.

THE ESSENTIAL NATURE OF RELIGION.

STRAUSS closes his diatribe against faith in immortality in words which sum up his prin-

---

* Gott und die Natur, 2 Aufl. 330 seq.

ciple: "Nothing is immaterial except that which is not at all."* After that we might expect that to his second question, "Have we religion still?" he would return as downright a negative as he has given to the first. Materialists, at least, who are consistent with their principles, have constantly denied religion, unconditionally and in every aspect. STRAUSS is not ready for that. He begins once more his search into "the essential character" of religion. He justifies SCHLEIEMACHER's derivation of religion from the feeling of absolute dependence. But he also discovers that "FEUERBACH is right in "saying: The origin, in fact the very essence "of religion is desire. Had man no desires he "would have no gods. What man desires to "be, but is not, he makes into his god; what "he would like to have, but cannot secure for "himself, his god is to secure for him. It is "not, therefore, simply the dependence in which "he finds himself, but the need also of counter-"acting it, of setting himself over against it, in "freedom once more, from which religion arises "among men."† At an earlier point in his argument STRAUSS approves of the Epicurean the-

---

* Alt. u. Neu. Gl. Sechst. Aufl. 134
† P. 153, Sechst. Aufl. 137.

ory, that fear is the mother of religion. Now he approves of FEUERBACH's theory that the origin and the very essence of religion is desire. Are we to understand by this that the dread of hunger and want is identical with the desire of man to be what his god is, or what he imagines his god to be? And is this desire capable of being harmonized with the feeling of absolute dependence? Is it not a contradiction in the adjective, first to depress man to the level of the animal, who lives and cares only for the gratification of the wants of the senses, and then to take this very same being, man, in the very same relation, to wit, in the relation to religion, and endow him with the desire for a loftier being, the desire for divine perfection, power and freedom? Is it not just as contradictory to devise the very same phenomenon from two sources which are diametrically opposite—the feeling of dependence, and the need of freedom? Assuredly if man hides within him antitheses like these, if man have this duality of nature, he cannot be put upon the same plane with the rest of beings.

IX.

THE PERMANENT IN RELIGION. MAN, AND THE UNIVERSE.

To the acknowledgment of this STRAUSS himself is finally brought. He allows religion to stand as a distinguishing mark of human nature in its essential character. Only, " religion with us is no longer what it was with our fathers." It no longer involves faith in the existence of a God, and faith in the immortality of the soul. Its origin, and its essence is rather a "recognition of the universe," though it be but of a very narrow part of it. "We perceive in the
" world a restless alternation. In this alterna-
" tion, however, we soon discover something
" permanent, we discover order and law. We
" perceive in nature violent antitheses, and fear-
" ful conflicts; but we find that the existence
" and unison of the whole is not destroyed by
" them, but is, on the contrary, preserved. We
" perceive further a graduation, a development
" of the higher from the lower, of the delicate
" from the coarse, of the mild from the harsh.
" We find, besides, that we are, ourselves, ad-
" vanced both in our personal and social life in
" proportion as we succeed in subjecting to

" rule what is arbitrarily shifting within us and
" around us, in proportion as from the lower,
" we develop the higher, from the harsh develop
" the tender. To this sort of things, when we
" encounter it in the circle of human life, we
" give the name, rational and good. What we
" perceive in correspondence with it in the world
" around us we cannot help calling by the same
" names. And as, besides, we feel ourselves ab-
" solutely dependent on this world, as we derive
" our existence and the controlling influence of
" our being from it alone, we are compelled to
" regard it in its total notion, or as the universe,
" as also the primal source of all that is rational
" and good. From the fact that the rational and
" good in the human race proceeds from con-
" sciousness and will, the old religion drew the
" inference, that whatever we find in the broad
" world correspondent with these qualities must
" also have proceeded from a conscious and
" voluntary author. We have abandoned this
" sort of syllogism; we no longer regard the
" world as the work of an absolute, rational,
" and beneficent person, but as the working-
" place of the rational and the good. It is to
" our view no longer planned by a Supreme
" Reason, but planned on supreme reason. We
" must, indeed, in this view also, put into the

"cause what lies in the effect; what comes out
"of it, must have been in it. But this is noth-
"ing more than the limitation of our human
"mode of conception; the universe is, in fact,
"at one and the same time cause and effect, ex-
"ternal and internal. .... It is consequently
"that something on which we feel ourselves
"absolutely dependent. It is in no wise or man-
"ner a coarse domineering power, before which
"we bow in dumb resignation, but is at once
"order and law, reason and goodness, to which
"we commit ourselves in loving trust. And yet
"more, as we perceive in ourselves that draw-
"ing to the rational and good, which we believe
"we perceive in the world, as we find that we
"are the beings by whom it is felt and recog-
"nized, in whom it is to become personal, we
"feel ourselves, in our inmost soul, in affinity
"with that on which we find ourselves depend-
"ent—in our very dependence we find ourselves
"free; in our feeling for the universe pride is
"mingled with humility, joy with resignation."*

---

* P. 136 seq. Sechst. Aufl. 142 seq.

X.

THE NEW FAITH.

This "feeling for the universe" is STRAUSS's religion, the "new faith," which is to set aside the old faith.

STRAUSS himself expresses a doubt whether "persons" will allow this feeling to pass for religion. And beyond doubt "persons," that is, the great majority of those who associate a distinct notion with the word "religion," will decline to bestow it on this new faith. But STRAUSS cares little for names, and hence to the question, Whether "we" have religion still? his reply is, "Yes or no, just as persons are inclined to take it."

To us also the name is a matter of little moment, but the more do we attach importance to the true notion and the grounds on which it is established. We do not deny that STRAUSS possesses the feeling for the universe to which he lays claim, nor that he believes in the correctness of the conceptions out of which that feeling springs up in his breast. But we do maintain that these conceptions and assumptions are not only extremely vague and superficial, but that they contradict each other in manifold respects, as they also contradict the assertions involving his whole principle, which he makes in various other places. It is one marked feature that what is inexorably demanded by logic, he treats as "the limitation of our human mode of conception." He acknowledges that "we must put into the cause also, what lies in the effect," and consequently that if the world be "the working-place of the rational and good," we are *compelled* to suppose that for the rational and good which is effected there must also be a cause; and that we cannot avoid conceiving of the cause as different from the effect, the external as different from the internal. But inasmuch as this pitiful logical necessity is nothing more than a limitation of our human mode of conception, the universe is, "*at one and the same time*, cause and effect, external and internal." We are "*compelled*," indeed, to distinguish the two, and consequently are *unable* to think one and the same thing, as at one and the same time, cause and effect; but as this is merely the result of the limitation just spoken of, we totally disregard it, and proclaim the truth, which we have no power of thinking, proclaim it in words, destitute of all meaning, but none the less sonorous! STRAUSS does not consider that we may with equal propriety, speak of the truth of wooden iron, or of a four-cornered triangle, and, to come more closely home to him still, that the doctrine of the Trinity, which he so decidedly contests, on the ground that three cannot be one, can make a direct appeal to him, and can, with equal propriety, assert that this logical distinction of one and three is nothing more than a limitation of our human mode of thinking.

XI.

THE DISCOVERY.

The "discovery" that in the world there is not only order and law, but also that there is a "development of the higher from the lower, of "the delicate from the coarse, of the mild from "the harsh," and that this higher something, this delicacy, mildness or tenderness, when we find it in the circle of human life, is the "rational and good," this discovery is the basis of STRAUSS's new religion. The "we," in whose name he speaks, will no doubt rest with entire satisfaction in this discovery. But the scientific investigator, and especially the philosophical thinker, have the preposterous whim of declining to be put off with mere words; they will insist on asking after their meaning and force. And we ask, accordingly, what is that "higher something, that delicacy and mildness," of which STRAUSS is speaking? In what way is it to be distinguished from the low, the coarse, the harsh? As STRAUSS leaves us without a reply, we should be compelled, on this ground, were there no other, to deny that the attempt at establishing the new religion has any scientific value whatever. Higher and lower, coarse and delicate, harsh and mild, are designations whose tenor is so indefinite, so relative and slight, that unless they be accurately defined they amount to nothing. And why is it that the delicate, mild little squirrel is more rational, and is better than the coarse, rough swine? Why is the humming-bird better than the owl? Why is the butterfly better than the cockchafer? Why is the rose better than the thistle? The professed materialist, to whom everything is blind necessity and conformity to law, has no right to make distinctions either between higher and lower, between coarse and delicate, or between the rational and irrational, the good and the bad. What is the product of blind necessity is equally high and low, equally rational and irrational, equally good and bad, because it is neither the one nor the other. The fact that materialism does not see the contradiction in which it involves itself, in imposing on a blind, unconscious, unthinking necessity, the adjustment of a development of a higher something out of a lower, the controlling with reason and goodness, this fact allows of but one solution. The solution is found in the superficiality and lack of thought which seem to cleave inevitably to that system. For such a control as this view concedes, *presupposes* of necessity a *distinction* between the higher and the lower, the good and the bad. The lower must from the beginning have been so *designed* that the higher could shape itself out of it; it must consequently have been originally placed in *relation* to the higher something, and must have been determined in conformity with it. But how does it come to avoid the irrational, or to carry on a training which results in the rational, inasmuch as there is no distinction whatever between the two? The rational and irrational are not things which the hand can grasp; there is no such thing as rational or irrational matter. The rational and irrational is nothing at all material, nothing phenomenal, nothing addressing our sense perceptions. It is a something which is to be inferred from certain given conceptions. The rational is therefore itself conception, it is *nothing but* conception, which we shape to ourselves mainly from our own attitude, our willing and thinking over our conduct in its ethical relations. The power of deriving this conception from the facts of consciousness, and of thinking, willing and acting in conformity with it, we call reason. Where there is no thinking, willing and acting, in an ethical respect, there is consequently no reason; the use of the term is an abuse. Of the reason of nature and the rationality of nature we know nothing at all originally. We transfer them to nature, because we believe we recognize in it a similar bearing of things and events to each other, a similar order and harmony, an activity involving plan and aim, proceeding from similar motives, directed to the preservation of the whole, and to the promotion of the interests of the individual parts. But in this very process we impute to nature the *conception* of the rational, and of a thinking, willing and acting derived from *that conception*, and we can talk no longer of blind necessity. The consistent materialist who knows what he is talking of, is necessarily a casualist in the strict sense, that is, he holds that the seeming conformity to law, the order, the rationality, whether in nature or in human life, are either mere seeming and illusion, or the fortuitous result of fortuitous combinations of fortuitously existing matter, out of fortuitously occurring operations, which just as fortuitously may at any moment, separate, fall to pieces, or enter into new combinations. If in spite of all this he is determined to have religion still, he has nothing left to worship but insensate Chance.

XII.

THE GOOD AND THE BAD.

And what right furthermore has STRAUSS to draw a distinction between good and bad? We can only speak of good in the ethical sense on the assumption of the freedom of the will. And a being in absolute dependence on nature, and its laws, cannot even in the most contracted sense be called free. It is certainly beyond all comprehension how such a being can ever go so far as to "react" against his "absolute dependence," and strive after freedom. Certainly this striving is a gross error, a treacherous illusion, and that reaction can be nothing more than a purely impotent outrage. The good in STRAUSS's new religion can therefore be nothing more than the feeling of pleasure, the agreeable, the useful. With it coincides then, as a matter of course, the rational, for these two notions STRAUSS identifies. His only reason, therefore, for regarding the delicate, mild and tender as good, is that he supposes that these are more agreeable, delightful and beneficial than their opposites. The great majority of men, however, find themselves much more comfortable in what is gross and coarse, than in what is fine and tender; they regard a coarse license as far more agreeable than subjection to law, and the bad, as in many cases, more useful than the good. With what right then does STRAUSS maintain that the opposite is good? When the sensuous material man of STRAUSS's description finds himself pained by the law, order and reason, which sway in the universe, why should he persist in calling them good? In fact we have once more a gross contradiction of STRAUSS's own premises when he pronounces the "coarse domineering power," the coarse dissoluteness, to be evil, while on the other hand, the "resignation" to the order and reason which sway in the universe is good. He even goes beyond this and defines man as the being in whom the rational and good "is to become personal." Yet, after all this, he gainsays the claim of this very being, man, to soul, freedom, morality. A being "absolutely dependent" on nature and its laws, *cannot* feel that nature's power is "a coarse domineering," *cannot* subject himself to it, either in "dumb resignation," or "with loving trust." For if no real possibility of transgressing the law, coexist with the law, subjection under law is no *self*-subjection, no *self*-surrender, but is simply an unconditioned *state* of subjection.

XIII.

STRAUSS IN CONFLICT WITH CONSISTENT MATERIALISM; PESSIMISM; SCHOPENHAUER, VON HARTMANN.

The consistent materialists, therefore, who do not find in the world embodied reason and goodness, are regarded by STRAUSS as his opponents, though in other respects they are in complete harmony with his principles. He therefore resorts to sharp weapons in his battle with the Pessimism of SCHOPENHAUER and VON HARTMANN. He finds in them, as he does in every pessimistic view of the world, "the grossest contradiction." For "if this world is a thing
" which had better not be, then, forsooth, the
" thinking of philosophers, which forms a part
" of this world, is a thinking which had better
" not be thought. The pessimist philosopher
" does not notice how, more than all, he declares
" as bad his own thinking, which declares the
" world to be bad; but if a thinking which de-

"clares the world to be bad is bad thinking,
"then it follows, on the contrary, that the world
"is good. Optimism may, as a rule, make its
"own task a little too easy; and in this aspect
"Schopenhauer's proof of the tremendous part
"played by pain and evil in the world are en-
"tirely in place; but every true philosophy is
"necessarily optimistic, as in any other theory
"it denies its own right to existence (it saws off
"the branch on which it is sitting)."* This
criticism is entirely convincing. But does it
not involve Strauss's own philosophy and the
new religion he has built on it? If nothing but
the delicate, the mild, the tender is good, is
there not at least as much of the gross, the
coarse, the harsh in the world? And if good
be no more than the secular well-being of man,
who is thoroughly earthy and material, is not
every one with whom, in his own estimation,
things have gone badly on the whole, or at least
not as well as they ought to have gone, entirely
justified in maintaining that the subsisting regulation of the world is bad? Is he not at least
on as defensible ground as that taken by the
optimist with the opposite view? To say nothing, then, of the internal contradictions of

---

* P. 142, Sechst. Aufl. 147.

Strauss's view, does he not make his own task a little "too easy" when he grounds his optimism on the "discoveries" which have been stated?

XIV.

"WHAT IS OUR APPREHENSION OF THE UNIVERSE?"

After Strauss has laid the basis of religion in general, only on our knowledge of the world, and the feeling which springs from it, he attempts in the third division an answer to the question, "What is our apprehension of the universe?" He applies himself forthwith to the knotty, much-mooted problem, whether the universe is to be conceived of as infinite or finite. He decides that it is infinite, but again without telling us what he means by infinity. And yet the old controversy was caused by a failure on the part of the combatants to attempt to come to an understanding in advance in reference to the notion of the infinite. If we take the word in a purely negative sense, and such a sense the word itself involves, it is evident that the infinite, as the negation of the finite, or limited, not only *presupposes* the finite of which it is the negation, but is in itself nothing but negation, and is, consequently, *nothing*. To speak of a primordial something, infinite in itself in this sense, whether we suppose it to be the Deity or the universe, is consequently a contradiction in the adjective. The finite, it is true, involves also a negation; it is, indeed, a positive, an existent by another existent, but with a negation, a bound or limitation, attached to it, and is, consequently, a being which in itself involves a non-being. The first problem, consequently, is to define, to determine the notion of the finite. This involves the solution of the old Eleatic question, How can being coexist with non-being? Had STRAUSS thoroughly reflected on this question, he would have discovered that no answer to it is possible, except by the notion of distinction and of distinguishing activity as the fundamental and primal activity of all thinking, or consciousness, and as the determining primal force of all that is in being. Instead of this, without anything further, he proclaims the infiniteness of the world, and imagines that he has solved the problem by making a distinction between " world in the absolute sense, that is, " the universe, and world in the relative sense " in which it has a plural." Thereupon he maintains that " though it is true that every " world in the latter sense, through parts of the " totality in its widest compass, has its limita- " tion in space as it has its beginning and end

" in time, yet the universe spreads itself forth
" and maintains its continuity illimitably, alike
" through all space and all time."* "Conse-
" quently not only our earth, but our solar system
" also, and every other part of the totality of the
" universe, has at one period been what it no
" longer is [in this sort did not exist at all], and
" will one day cease to be as it is now," but as
to the universe " there never was a time when
" it was not, a time when there was in it no
" distinction of celestial bodies, no life, no rea-
" son. All this, if it was not in one part of the
" totality, was in another part, and had ceased
" to be in a third part; here it was coming into
" being, there it was in full subsistence, in a
" third place it was passing away; the universe
" is an infinite complex of worlds in all the
" stadia of origin and transition, and because of
" this eternal revolution and alternation pre-
" serves itself in eternal absolute fulness of
" life."† This train of thought is essentially that
of KANT. STRAUSS has, in his own opinion, improved upon it, but in reality has made it worse
in the mending, by throwing out the notion of
creation and of God, and with this he imagines

---

* Sechst. Aufl. 152.
† P. 148 seq. Sechst. Aufl. 153.

he has disposed of the whole matter. But is not an "*un*limited" whole, made up of nothing but *limited* parts, be they celestial bodies or atoms, a glaring contradiction in the adjective? Is there not a palpable contradiction in this description of a totality, in which at *every* time, and consequently at *one and the same time*, a part coming into being, subsists and has subsisted by the side of one which has already come into being? The part which has come into being must, nevertheless, also at one time have been in the course of coming into being, must consequently have been in being before the part which is just coming into being, and consequently as something in actual being cannot be associated as *simultaneous* with what is just coming into being. In other words, just as little as we are in a condition to think of an infinite whole with nothing but finite parts, that is, a finite infiniteness or an infinite finiteness, just as little can we think of an activity which is in a purely negative sense eternal, that is, absolutely without beginning. For the act proceeding from such an activity must likewise be simply without beginning, as an activity without something to do is no activity. But we can only think of the act as the *result* of the activity, the activity only as *prior* to the act. The act *begins* consequently of necessity by and with the activity; an act without beginning is a contradiction in the adjective, as that would mean an act without activity, an effect without a cause. It follows also that an activity without beginning is a contradiction in the adjective, for that, as an act without beginning, is impossible, and would be an activity without an act, a cause without an effect. For this very reason then we can conceive a beginning which *is* positive, the absolute antecedent of all origin and of all that is originated, of all doing and of all that comes to pass, and which on this very account *has* no beginning in another. In fact we are compelled to accept such an absolute antecedent, inasmuch as the unbeginning, the simple negation of beginning, involves as its own *presupposition* the very thing it denies, and consequently involves the thought of absolute beginning. If STRAUSS, then, does not mean to insist that a finiteness without end, an act without activity, is conceivable, he will have to abandon the infiniteness and eternity of his universe, and will have to concede the *positively* infinite, as that which sets all limitation and bounds, all greatness, and all measure (by distinction), and the *positively* eternal as the absolute antecedent of all origin and of all that is originated, of all doing and of all that comes to pass, and hence of the world itself.

XV.

THE COSMOGONY OF KANT AND LA PLACE.

In order to show how we may apprehend the origination of a world, in the "relative" sense of the word, without the interference of a higher and divine power, STRAUSS goes on to develop in his own fashion the familiar hypothesis by which KANT and LA PLACE explained the rise and development of our solar system. [The proof I have presented that this self-origination and self-development without a *primum movens et determinans*—a primary mover and determiner—is inconceivable,* STRAUSS, as a matter of course, again fails to notice. He notices, nevertheless, some of the facts which are in decided conflict with the hypothesis, but he puts them all aside with the weighty remark: "This belongs to those inexactnesses in the results of nature of which KANT speaks!"†] It would far transcend the proper limits of an article in a Review to follow with our criticism each step of STRAUSS's exposition. We shall confine our notices therefore to a few untenable positions taken by him in the sphere of the natural sci-

---

* Ulrici: Gott u. die Natur, Zweit. Aufl. 337–353.
† Alt. u. Neu. Glaub. 158.

ences. It is inadmissible to argue from the shortening of the track of a comet (Enke's) to the orbit of the planets, the shortening of which has not to this hour been established by any reliable observation. For out of the demonstrated fact of the division of Biela's comet, in 1845, it is evident that under some circumstances the comets may be diminished in bulk. The comet thus divided did not reappear in 1866, nor in 1872, when it could not have failed to be observed. Instead of that, in November, 1872, there was observed a fall of a great number of shooting stars, which previously had moved in the track about the sun in which Biela's comet had kept, rendering it highly probable that the comet had gone to fragments, and that under certain conditions of the masses of matter of which comets are composed, they may be completely sundered so as to go to pieces. With the diminution of the mass the track is necessarily shortened. Strauss is mistaken when he goes on to assert: "Assuming, with "Kant and La Place, the mass of nebular ex- "tended matter as the relative primal matter of "our planetary system, we conceive, even if we "suppose it to be derived from a previous pro- "cess of combustion, that it was completely "cooled because of its extreme disgregation."

Conformably with this we have to assume that the scattered atoms "did not attain heat and "luminosity until they approximated under the "law of gravitation." For it is established by natural science, that the ponderable forms of matter—apart from the few permanent gases—are resolved into masses of vapor, or pass into "disgregation" only in consequence of increasing heat, and require sustained heat to be kept in that condition. With the beginning of the cooling, gravitation and chemical attraction come into corresponding activity. That the primary matter should be "completely cooled off," and should yet be a nebulous mass, is a thing which natural science shows to be impossible. It is equally false that "the revolving "motion is natural to a spherical mass consist-"ing of matter in the form of vapor or of fluid." On the contrary, it is a universally acknowledged theorem that no ponderable mass simply *of itself*, without a force moving it, sets itself in motion, either of a rotary character or of any other.

XVI.

ORIGIN OF LIFE UPON EARTH—GENERATIO ÆQUIVOCA. ORGANIC AND INORGANIC.

With a quick turn STRAUSS finishes up the development of our terrestrial globe, and goes on to the question in regard to the origination of organisms or "living substances."* Though he admits that "in consequence of the difficulty of "making conclusive experiments, a general deci- "sion has not yet been reached," he yet decides without hesitation for the *generatio æquivoca* or *spontanea*. He reduces the question to this shape: "Whether it is possible that an indi- "vidual organism, even of the least perfect sort, "can arise in any other way than through its "own like? can arise, to wit, by chemical or "morphologic processes, which take place not "in the egg, or in the womb, but in other forms "of matter, in organic or inorganic fluids."†

Virchow says that all known facts give their testimony *against* spontaneous generation in our day. To meet this Strauss resorts to "entirely "extraordinary conditions, in the era of the "greater revolutions of the earth," that out of them life may come forth, "of course, in its yet incompletest form," of which the Bathybius and Moneres are examples. This coming forth con- sists in the "special movement of the matter, "through which, from time to time, a part of "collective matter withdraws, from the ordinary "course of its movements, into special organico-

---

* P. 167, Sechst. Aufl. 171.
† P. 169, Sechst. Aufl. 173.

"chemical combinations. In this state it remains "for a time, and then reverts to the general re- "lations of movement."* "If the question be "properly regarded," continues Strauss, "it "does not involve the creation of something new, "but only the bringing of existent forms of mat- "ter and forces into another species of combina- "tion and movement, and for this a sufficient "occasion may be found, in the conditions of "primeval time, so totally diverse from those of "the present, the wholly different temperature, "and of atmospheric composition, and similar "causes."†

Strauss forgets that but a few pages before he has observed: "The geology of our day is in- "clined to construe the details of the formation "of our earth far more in accordance with ordi- "nary method, far more in accordance with what "we see at present in the course of nature."‡ And, in fact, the geology of our day, subsequent to Lyell, is not only "inclined" thus "to con- strue" the details, but has pretty clearly demon- strated that it is precisely in this way things actually came to pass. The appeal to "the con- ditions of primeval time," so totally diverse from

---

* Virchow.
† Sechst. Aufl. 175.
‡ Sechst. Aufl. 171.

those of the present, is an evasion which is no longer allowable, especially as it is an established fact, that a "wholly different temperature," that is, one higher than the tropical, the highest degree now known, as well as a "different atmospheric composition," does not further organic life, but, on the contrary, destroys it. But were we to grant that life consists only in that special movement of a part of "collective matter," and that the conditions of primeval time furnish a sufficient occasion for the origination of that movement, the question still remains to be answered, Why is it but "a part?" Why does not the entire collective matter, at disposal, and fitted for this special movement, enter on it? Another question forces itself on us. Why does this part remain only "for a time" in these special organico-chemical combinations, and then revert to the general relations of movement? Besides, it is false that the "living substance" consists merely in a special organico-chemical combination of matter. On the contrary, the question is urgent, How can an organico-chemical combination of diverse atoms, oxygen, hydrogen, nitrogen, carbon, and others, come to *live?* To reach this involves more than the entrance of this or that set of atoms into an organico-chemical combination by means of special movement, and then remaining for a time in the combination. Sugar, urine, cyanogen, ethal, and other substances, are organico-chemical combinations, but they are not organisms, they are not "living substances." Every organism, even of the very lowest grade, even the Bathybius and the Moneres, exercises distinct functions. It is compelled to preserve itself, to nourish itself, to keep off certain matter from itself, to draw other matter to it, to take it into itself, to propagate itself. Without this it would not subsist for a moment. With the cessation of this spontaneity, itself and its kind would cease to exist. These functions, these "special" movements are found in organized matter only, never in unorganized. It is these, not what are called the organico-chemical combinations of certain forms of matter which constitute the most general and essential marks of every "living substance," and of the living substance *only*. They too, then, must have a cause. And as they are "special" processes, deviating from the general conditions of movement, as it is an established fact that the chemical substances within the organic combinations exhibit different activities from those they possess outside of them, we are compelled to suppose a "special" cause for these special processes. Whether we call this cause vital force, or give it whatever name we please, so long as the chemist fails in generating in his laboratory, from purely inorganic substances, a "living substance," a solitary organism, even of the very lowest order, so long will he fail to remove either the distinction between an organism and a mere chemical combination of matter, whether of an organic or inorganic nature, or the distinction between a living being and a complicated machine. So long, at least, will every man cling to that distinction, who does not one day acknowledge and the next day deny the law of causality, as a legitimate law of thought.

XVII.

ORIGIN OF SPECIES. THE DARWINIAN THEORY.

In the much-mooted question of the origin of species, STRAUSS, as has already been intimated, is an enthusiastic adherent of DARWIN. He acknowledges, indeed, that the Darwinian theory is "still extremely imperfect;" "it leaves infi-"nitely much unexplained, and in the unex-"plained are not merely subordinate matters, "but what are really chief and cardinal points; "he rather hints at solutions which may be pos-"sible in the future, than gives them himself." Still STRAUSS claims that the theory is a grand advance, full of significance. For DARWIN "has "opened the door through which the happier "world that is to follow us will throw out all "miracle never to return. Whoever is aware "how much hangs on the idea of miracle, will "thank him for this as one of the greatest bene- "factors of our race."*

It is an extraordinary thing that the great critic never turns the edge of his criticism against himself, his own opinions and prejudices, his own sympathies and antipathies! It is not difficult to comprehend that the author of "The Life of Jesus" has no affection for theological miracles. But is it allowable, for the gratification of this antipathy, to laud as the greatest and most beneficent of discoveries, a theory which leaves unexplained "what are really chief and cardinal points," and which consequently is, in fact, *no* theory at all, only because in STRAUSS's judgment it does away with the idea of miracle? Is it admissible, in favor of such a theory, to confound notions which are widely different? Yet this is the very thing which STRAUSS does. Led by this antipathy he confounds the theological miracles, such for example as that of the wedding-feast

---

* P. 177, Sechst. Aufl. 181.

at Cana, and others of its class, with the miracles of natural science; that is, with the incomprehensible fact which natural science is incapable of explaining.

The older theory assumed that the lowest genera and species of organic being arose from a force not assignable to nature, consequently, a supernatural cause, a metaphysical force. DARWIN maintains that organic being involves separate evolutions, and that the higher have arisen from the lower by gradual transformation. The old view certainly was not able to explain the precedency in question; it was not in a condition to demonstrate the activity and the mode of operation of that metaphysical potency. But DARWIN's theory also leaves unexplained "what are really chief and cardinal points," and must in addition leave uncomprehended that "special" movement as the first cause of the chemical organic combinations.

To this theory there clings quite enough beyond comprehension and beyond explication. If each and every thing which we can neither comprehend nor explain be a miracle, then are we, in spite of all that has been attained by the investigation of nature, still compassed by downright miracles. Or is STRAUSS, perhaps, able to tell us how the force of gravitation can put bodies into motion at a distance of thousands and thousands of miles?—a fact, which as is well known, the illustrious NEWTON pronounced as beyond the power of imagination. Or does STRAUSS, perchance, know how to give us a statement "as to the cause of the diversity of "the chemical elements, the nature of the force "which occasions the chemical combinations, "the laws which control the chemical metamor- "phoses," things of which KEKULÉ* says, "our "chemistry possesses *no sort* of exact knowl- "edge." Can he bring within our grasp the mode in which light (the luminiferous force) sets the ethereal atoms into transversal undula- tions, and how this movement transmits itself in exactly the opposite direction in longitudinal undulation, albeit physics, as EISENLOHR con- fesses, "can furnish nothing certain in regard "to the causes of the wave-movement of the "ether effected by the surface of the sun and of "the fixed stars." Or is he, perchance, able to explain the extremely diverse operations of elec- tricity, which EISENLOHR styles, "the *unknown* "cause of a vast multitude of phenomena." Especially is STRAUSS at all prepared to explain the law of inductive electricity; to wit, "that

---

* Lehrbuch der Organischen Chemie, p. 95.

"the induced stream, on approximation to the "primary stream, shows a tendency opposite "to it, but on being removed from the pri- "mary stream assumes the same direction with "it?" These are but a few of the unanswered questions, of the unexplained and uncomprehended facts in the sphere of the natural sciences. If STRAUSS be not able to solve them, he is bound to confess that on the first point, even that "happier aftertime" has exceedingly little prospect of "getting rid of" miracle, as he uses the word.

After this allusion, in passing, to the supremest benefactor of humanity, STRAUSS presents us with a very popular, excessively superficial delineation or description of the Darwinian theory, without ever mentioning, to say nothing of attempting to answer, the many and weighty objections which have been raised against it, even by writers of high authority in the natural sciences. He might have found these in HUBER's work.* This is not the place to estimate the weight of these objections. We propose no more than to point out the utterly uncritical course pursued by the renowned critic.

---

* J. HUBER: Die Lehre Darwin's &c. München, 1873.

He accepts the Darwinian doctrine with childlike trust. He believes in it in spite of the considerations of various kinds, the grounds of doubt, the confutations which rise against it. He does the very thing which he charges on the "devout believers," whom he so despises and assails. This is the way they treat his critical objections and assaults. He believes in Darwin's doctrine partly on authority, partly because it suits his personal opinions and views!

XVIII.

THE APE AND MAN. MAN AND THE ANIMALS, THEIR AFFINITIES AND DISTINCTIONS.

From the theory of descendence it inevitably results, according to Strauss, that man is derived from the ape, if not from a species now existing, yet from a pretended species which has become extinct. In a popular treatment of the subject he presents the grounds for this indisputably logical inference from the theory. He launches out into testimonies for the great intellectual endowments of the animals, or at least of particular kinds of animals. He concurs also with Darwin in the opinion that in the higher animals "the beginnings of moral feeling"* reveal themselves. Not only are the instincts of animals which direct themselves "to the care of their young, the anxiety, toil "and sacrifice through which they pass for their "young," to be looked upon as "revealing a tendency to the higher moral faculties," but "a "sort of feeling of honor and of conscience, is "scarcely to be mistaken in the nobler horses "and dogs which have been well cared for." He adds, indeed, that the conscience of a dog "is "not entirely without justice referred to the "rod," but, he asks, "whether the case is very "different with the rougher class of men?" That means that the human conscience, and consequently human morality, is to be referred to the rod. For that the earliest men, as they descend from the race of apes, must have been not merely "rough," but excessively rough, is indubitably certain, inasmuch as it is an indubitable consequence of the theory of descendence. But apart from the fact that this pretended conscience of the horse and dog is to be referred to the rod and whip *only*, STRAUSS overlooks the fact, that the whip must be at hand, and that there must be somebody to apply it, if the conscience is to be brought into

---

* Sechst. Aufl. 208.

being or aroused. Man uses the rod on the dog. Who is there to use it on man? Another man, of course. The first man then who employed the rod to arouse a conscience in another must of necessity have possessed conscience and moral feeling, in and of himself, without the aid of the rod. The question inevitably arises, why does one dog never use the conscience-making rod on another dog? Is it perhaps because dogs possess only "a sort" of conscience? But apart from the fact that STRAUSS does not devote a word of explanation as to what this "sort," be it species or be it variety, may be, he must in any case acknowledge that the conscience of a dog or the conscience of a man, which is aroused and controlled by the rod, is very different not only "in quantity," but in quality too, from the conscience which is self-awakened and self-evolved. His first duty then is to show that the two are nevertheless identical in principle and character. To do this he must show that the nursing and feeding of their young by the higher orders of animals, are to be regarded as a token of moral feeling, or of the higher moral faculties. This is the more imperative, as it is well known that as soon as their young are grown, as soon as, in the case of birds, the brood is fledged, not only does the care cease at once, but there is a change to the very reverse. They drive away their young, they enter into the same combat and struggles with them as with others for food, all of which furnishes evidence of the purely instinctive character of the whole. Until STRAUSS succeeds in doing this, we shall feel justified in finding the solution of his assertions in that mingling and confounding of notions, which clings to materialism like an endemic sickness, which seems to attack every one who gives himself up to that system.

XIX.

THE SOUL.

The "incarnation" of the ape leads the defender of that view by a very natural transition to the contested question concerning the soul. STRAUSS stands fast by the colors of the new faith. He denies without qualification any sort of specific difference between body and soul. He claims, if not to have settled the question, yet at least to have broken the pathway to a solution of it, by proclaiming the doctrine of sensualism, and referring all thinking to sensation, and starts the question: "If under certain "conditions movement is transmuted into

"warmth, why may there not be conditions
"under which it is transmuted into sensation?
"We have the necessary conditions, the appa-
"ratus for this in the brain and nervous system
"of the higher animals, and in those organs,
"which in the lower orders of animals supply
"their place. On the one side the nerve is
"touched and put into motion, on the other
"there is a respondent sensation, a perception;
"a process of thinking springs up. And con-
"versely on the way outward the sensation and
"the thought set the members of the body in
"motion. HELMHOLTZ says: 'In the generation
"'of warmth by friction and concussion the
"'motion of the entire mass passes over into a
"'motion of its minutest particles, and con-
"'versely, by the generation of mechanical
"'power by warmth the motion of the minutest
"'particles passes over into a motion of the
"'whole mass.' I ask then, is this essentially
"different from the view I am urging? Is not
"what I have asserted but the sequel to the
"statement of HELMHOLTZ?"* HELMHOLTZ
himself would certainly answer this question
with a decided No. STRAUSS forgets that what
we call warmth does not exist, physically, in in-

---

* P. 206 seq. Sechst. Aufl. 211, 212.

organic nature at all. The word designates a distinct sensation, which under certain circumstances is present and comes to our consciousness. Physics has demonstrated that the rise of it is conditioned by distinct movements of the ethereal atoms, and in a certain respect of the ponderable atoms, the " minutest portions " of a mass, that is, it arises when these movements meet nerves sensible to them, capable of excitation by them. Warmth, therefore, *presupposes* a being capable of sensation, endowed with sensibility. There exists consequently not the slightest analogy between the origination of sensation and those physical movements which pass from the masses to their minutest parts, and again from the parts to the mass. The minutest particles of air, when by compression or by the rays of the sun they are set into those motions, have sensation of warmth just as little as the particles of iron or silver in a state of fusion have it. For as the illustrious physiologist DONDERS observes, " The essential charac-
" ter of all forms of operation, and of the faculty
" of operation with which we are acquainted, is
" motion and condition of motion, and no man
" can shape to himself a conception, how out of
" motions, be they combined in any manner
" they may, consciousness or any psychical ac-

"tivity whatever can arise." Were it granted also that the nerves, if they are affected by those movements, went into a similar movement of their minutest particles—a theory which is far from having been proven—that does not involve any sensation of warmth. Du Bois-Reymond —an authority in natural science to whom Strauss now and then appeals—puts the point in question in these words: "What imaginable "connection is there, on the one side, between "distinct movements of distinct atoms in my "brain, and on the other, of facts primitive for "me, incapable of further definition, beyond all "possibility of denial, facts like these: I feel "pain, I feel pleasure, I taste something sweet, "I smell the aroma of a rose, I hear the tones "of the organ, I see something red—and the "assurance just as directly flowing from these "facts: Therefore I am?" Du Bois-Reymond regards the question also as unanswerable, and hence states the case more amply: "It is just "as incomprehensible throughout and forever, "that it should not be a matter of indifference "to a quantity of atoms of carbon, hydrogen, "nitrogen, oxygen and others, how they lie and "move, how they once lay and moved, and how "they are about to lie and move." It is not then at consciousness, not at free will we first reach "the limits of our knowledge of nature." Those insurmountable limits are already reached in "the problem of sense-perception."* Unless STRAUSS be prepared to perform what DU BOIS-REYMOND, in the name of natural science, pronounces impossible, unless he be prepared to answer this question, unless he can make it intelligible why, to a number of atoms of carbon, hydrogen and other substances, out of which the nerves in common with all the bodily organs consist, it should not be indifferent whether they were arranged in this or that combination—unless STRAUSS is prepared to do all this, the one-sided materialism to which he gives his adhesion is an hypothesis scientifically untenable, as valueless scientifically as any other purely subjective opinion, as valueless as any faith or any superstition you may be pleased to select. For if it be simply inconceivable how sensation and consciousness can arise from a mechanical movement or chemical combination of a number of atoms, the mental law of causality compels us to suppose that there is another cause for the existence of sensation, not a cause which operates in a merely mechanical or chemical way.

---

* Ueber die Grenzen des Naturerkennens, Vortrag, etc., Leipzig, Veit, 1872, p. 25 seq.

It compels us to distinguish the substances, the atoms endowed with the power of sensation from others which are invested with no more than physical and chemical forces. The former need by no means be purely immaterial; they may always possess physical and chemical forces in conjunction with the faculty of sensation, and may be subject to the operation of such forces. They may beside differ very much among each other. Nevertheless, as sentient beings, they stand over against the insentient in well-defined, insoluble antithesis. With justice, therefore, a special name has been given them—they are called "souls." Their actual existence contradicts the materialistic hypothesis, which acknowledges *nothing but* physical and chemical forces. This contradiction is so decided that none but philosophical dilettanti, who as a rule deal with logic in a very arbitrary fashion, or men who consciously or unconsciously are influenced by other than purely philosophical interests, can still cling to it.

XX.

STRAUSS'S APPEAL TO DU BOIS-REYMOND.

[In STRAUSS'S "Word at the close, designed as a preface to the later editions of his Old Faith and New Faith,"* he attempts to weaken the force of the statement we have quoted from Du Bois-Reymond, adapted as it is to shake the very foundation of his doctrine. This he does by appealing to Du Bois-Reymond himself, who does expressly acknowledge, that, in accordance with the known principle of investigation, to give the preference to the simpler conception of the cause of a phenomenon, until it be successfully confuted, we shall constantly find our thinking drawn toward the conjecture, that if we were only able to comprehend the essential character of matter and force—the perpetual incomprehensibleness of which, according to Du Bois-Reymond, forms the second, or rather the first limit of our knowledge of nature—we might perhaps understand also, how the substance which lies at their base, could under certain determinate conditions have sensations, desires, and thoughts.† Du Bois-Reymond certainly expresses himself about it in this sense toward the end of the publication we have cited. And it is a matter that requires no argument, that the investigator of nature, though he be unable to understand either the

---

* Ein Nachwort als Vorwort zu den neuen Auflagen meiner Schrift: Der Alte und der neue Glaubl. vierter Abdruck. Bonn, 1873.

† Quoted in Nachw. als. Vorw., 27, 28.

essential character of matter and force or the cause and origin of sensation, has no need to resort to dogmas and philosophemes about them, but unconfused by them can shape his own judgment as to the relations between spirit and matter. That is an open question to the investigator of nature as it is to everybody else. But the first question which arises is, whether these "views" be tenable, whether they be more than subjective opinions, more than mere "dogmas." But STRAUSS forgets, that DU BOIS-REYMOND not only regards the essential character of force and matter as purely incomprehensible, but expressly declares that the "atomistic representation" is "within certain defined limits," not only useful, but in fact indispensable to the investigation of nature, but that if it be extended into a general, unlimited theory, "it leads to hopeless contradiction."[*] It is this extension, however, into a general theory, exclusive in its character, allowing *nothing but* corporeal atoms, with their physico-chemical forces, which is the fundamental principle of materialism, or, to speak more accurately, of that particular materialistic hypothesis on which STRAUSS grounds his new faith. Any compend of Natural Science would have shown

---

[*] Grenze, etc., p. 9.

him that the atomistic-materialistic view of nature is in fact nothing more to the investigator of nature than a "hypothesis." But every hypothesis is condemned as scientifically untenable, just as soon as it shows that it is unable to explain, or involves itself in hopeless contradiction in the attempt to explain, the phenomena which it is framed and adopted to explain. This is a principle which the student of science holds as inviolable, as without it the way is opened to every fortuitous whimsy, every arbitrary fancy, in a word to the utter overthrow of science. If STRAUSS then be unable to confute these deliberate judgments of DU BOIS-REYMOND, and this he has not even attempted to do, he must concede that his new faith, based upon the exclusive materialistic hypothesis, is destitute of all scientific confirmation. His defence shows no more than that those judgments are very inconvenient to him. It creates the impression of a fruitless struggle and solicitude to break away from their annihilating results. It is unfortunate for him that the star, which has led him, already begins to pale, and that the materialistic doctrine already shows that it is a falling star rather than a true star. The rest of his "Word at the close" is nothing more than a defence of his religious and theological views against the numerous attacks made upon them from the most various quarters. We are consequently not concerned with it.]

XXI.

THE NOTION OF DESIGN, IN THE LIGHT OF NATURAL SCIENCE. PHILOSOPHY OF THE UNCONSCIOUS.

After this long ramble through the circle of the theories of the natural sciences, STRAUSS comes back to the investigation of the notion of design, in order that he may weaken the teleologic argument for the existence of God. DARWIN, who has opened the door for the expulsion of miracle, "has also removed from the expla-"nation of nature the notion of design, which "in the main coincides with the notion of mira-"cle." The notion of design, to wit, as STRAUSS in common with the older teleologists recognizes, involves consciousness thus far, that a spontaneous activity, conformable to a design, and yet without consciousness, is inconceivable. To speak, therefore, of an activity involving a final cause, setting before itself an aim, pursuing a plan, selecting the most fitting means, and yet to deny consciousness to such an activity, is simply self-contradiction. STRAUSS, therefore, rejects the philosophy of the unconscious, "the crotchet" of E. VON HARTMANN, which assumes an unconscious absolute, which as completely as

the conscious God of the teleological argument, with clearsighted wisdom, works by plan and choice, and determines all that is embraced in creation and the process of the universe. STRAUSS justly remarks that this theory is but the change of a word, from which results the ascription to a pretended unconsciousness, of things done, and of a course of action, which can belong only to a conscious being. "If we are to suppose," he continues, "that an Uncon-
"scious has brought to pass what appears to us
"in nature as conformable to design, I must
"conceive of its course of action in the case,
"as of that nature which belongs to the Un-
"conscious, that is, to speak with HELMHOLTZ,
"it must have swayed as a blind force of na-
"ture, and yet have brought to pass something
"which corresponds with a design. The newer
"investigation of nature in DARWIN has set us
"above this point of view." He has shown that the natural "need," the "struggle for exist-ence" has "gradually fashioned, developed, and
"perfected the organs of living things, in the
"way best adapted to satisfy the growing need,
"to maintain the struggle victoriously. Thus,
"in the course of the ages, ever higher and
"more perfect beings have resulted, more per-
"fect because more highly endowed with the
"faculties necessary to carry on the struggle in

" every direction under the most diverse condi-
" tions and relations."*

XXII.

THE SETTING ASIDE OF THE DOCTRINE OF FINAL CAUSES IN NATURE BY DARWIN.

Were we to grant that the Darwinian theory is completely justified and established—which it by no means is—it yet seems to us that the notion of design and miracle, which it puts out at one door, it lets in at another. Considered simply as a theory, it is, at least in the apprehension of it which STRAUSS furnishes, one-sided and inconsistent. For if it be nothing more than the diverse forms of need presenting themselves in the struggle for existence which controls organization, gradually shapes the organs, and then produces new genera and species, it follows that under some circumstances, *retro-gressions* may take place, and have taken place from the higher to the lower. The quadruped, for example, if a continent which had once been dry should be covered by vast inundations, will find himself confined to marshy, miry ground, and must consequently be able to turn back, and

---

* Page 213, seq. Sechst. Aufl. 218, seq.

must actually, under these circumstances, have been turned back into the reptile. The reptile, if it be forced to live in a comparatively narrow space, surrounded by great bodies of water, will by degrees, under the pressure of hunger, be compelled to resume the nature of the fish. The theory of descendence can therefore logically claim no more than a vacillation to and fro, according to circumstances, between higher and lower, between progression and retrogression. DARWIN himself consequently does not claim that there is a law of necessary rise and ultimate perfection in grade. Nevertheless, the theory, as the facts adduced in its support show, knows only of the rise and development of species ever higher and more perfect—a process which terminates in the appearing of a last, highest species, Man; and this is the very point which STRAUSS urges with special earnestness. To this inconsistency the theory moves involuntarily. The facts of natural science established by palæontology compel it so to move. But in so doing it falls helplessly again into the net of teleology, of which it imagined it had made a final disposition. For first of all, the primary lowest organisms must have been so planned that they were not merely in a general way "variable," but so that the variability of the individual members should have the definite tendency and inclination to vary from what was its original general type, in a manner adapted to its struggle for existence, and consequently to put forth organs fitted for and correspondent with the needs; in a word, organs formed or transformed in accordance with design. The same principle holds good in regard to the entire series of genera and species which gradually comes forth from the struggle for existence. Had mere accident controlled the result, nothing but unsuitable varieties might have arisen, or the suitable variations might have been so insignificant in number and importance that a higher organization never would have been reached. The varieties must furthermore be so constituted that they must not only be able permanently to preserve themselves without retrogression, but their suitably formed organs must also, of themselves, be developed and perfected; that is, not only their primary formation, but their development also, must be in accordance with design. But even the external circumstances and relations, the conditions of existence must have been originally so determined, and must in such sense change in the course of time, that other and yet other needs for the organism sprang from them. Otherwise the variations and new developments called forth by the need could neither take place nor attain permanence. It is required, therefore, that there should intervene a series of external conditions, circumstances and relations correspondent with the rise and preservation as well as with the sequence of the series which give themselves shape. Were it otherwise, no newer higher species could arise, and those which had arisen could not sustain themselves. Even in the domain of Geology, in the sequence of the stadia of the earth's development, there can be no domination of blind chance. Such a view is overthrown not only by the strength of the facts, but by the theory of descendence itself, as a theory. For chance can neither be in itself a theory, nor be brought into a theory. Theoretical or theorized chance is a contradiction in the adjective, in no respects different from wooden iron. If then we are compelled to accept a force which, on the one hand, so planned the organisms that in correspondence with the needs which from time to time arose, they varied themselves, and in higher and yet higher grades transformed, developed, and perfected themselves, and if this force, on the other hand, gave such direction to the external conditions, relations, and circumstances, that they went hand in hand with the formation and development of the species, made their changes in harmony with them, and through the entire processes cooperated subserviently to them, we think we have in this a power whose activity involves a final cause, an adaptation to design. For we cannot escape the implicit adoption of the view that the formation of ever higher, more perfect species was the aim pursued by that force in its activity, and that in conformity with this aim and its ultimate actualizing, it determined and arranged not only the earliest germs of organic life, but, never losing sight of that aim, the external conditions, circumstances, and relations necessary to it; in a word, that this force has selected, produced, and applied the means adapted to the attainment of its end. If, according to STRAUSS himself, such an activity is inconceivable, unless it be superintended and accompanied by a consciousness, then is the statement false that DARWIN has removed the notion of design from the explanation of nature, and has reduced to the sway of a "blind force of nature" what appears to us in nature as conformed to design. DARWIN, in fact, even if it be against his wish and knowledge, has acknowledged the notion of design, and has done nothing more than transfer it from the known end, the ultimate point of the organic creation, to the assumed beginnings, the earliest origin and development of that creation. [Neither STRAUSS nor DARWIN has weighed the question whether the order and conformity with law which control *in*organic nature do not presuppose the conscious, deliberate planning of a creative primitive force, and yet I believe I have clearly substantiated this position on the basis of natural science.*]

XXIII.

"HOW SHALL WE ORDER OUR LIFE?"

In spite of the partiality for the "blind" force of nature, and the partiality it involves for the lawless caprice of chance, STRAUSS is a decidedly ethical nature, a defender of the right and of the moral law, who, as it were, *contra naturam*, in defiance of nature, merely as the result of his ardor in his conflict against the orthodox theology—a conflict originally warranted in some particulars—has become a sensualist and materialist. That is made very clear in the last division of his work, in which he answers the question, "How shall we order our life?" Here we meet almost unobjectionable propositions, with which, though under reservation and sepa-

---

* Gott und die Natur, Zweit. Auflag. 420, 510 seq.

rating them entirely from their untenable foundation, we accord in the main. Especially is this the case with nearly all that he says on the political and social questions which so profoundly agitate our time. But it is just here we meet the grossest contradictions to his own premises. We shall cite only a few of the most striking ones. "The laws of the Decalogue," he says, in stating his views, "we acknowledge to "have proceeded from the recognized needs of "human society, needs suggested by experience, "and in this fact lies the basis of their immutable "obligation for us. Still in this commutation, "between an origin of the Decalogue in human "needs and an origin in divine Revelation, it is "impossible wholly to avoid the feeling that we "lose something. The divine origin of the laws "gave them sacredness; our view of their rise "seems to concede to them nothing more than "utility, or at most external necessity. There is "no way entirely to restore their sanctity except "by regarding their internal necessity, their com- "ing forth, not merely from social need, but from "the very nature or essential character of man."*
This means that if it could be shown that these laws originated in man's own nature we should

---

* Page 231, Sechst. Aufl. 235, 236.

have to regard them as possessing the same sanctity as if they proceeded from the holy will of God. But this would involve the assumption that if the nature of man is to be esteemed holy, sanctity is in some sense to be imputed to him. But in what sense does it pertain to him? And if it did pertain to him, it could only have proceeded from the social " necessity." For man himself is supposed to be through and through the creature of necessity. Through necessity, in the struggle for existence, man originally diverged from the race of " the primitive ape." It is the necessity of social life, as we were told, which in man in common with the beasts, originates and gives impulse to the moral feelings, the higher moral faculties. Man's development and consummation are originated, conditioned, and guided by necessity. How is it possible, then, that he should attain a nature or a being, which can be anything more exalted than an insoluble complex of manifold necessities, and of the faculties adapted to satisfy them?

XXIV.

THE PRIMARY PRINCIPLE OF MORALITY.

STRAUSS contests the correctness of SCHOPENHAUER'S opinion that pity is the sole spring of morality, and that consequently man can have no duties toward himself. In contesting this view he takes the case of a young man who has been striving diligently and persistently to form himself, morally. "Beside his intellectual and "moral endowments the young man feels in "himself other powers, powers in the sphere of "the senses. These, like the former, strive for "active exercise and expansion—reveal, indeed, "an energy and violence which that higher im- "pulse is not able to command. If, neverthe- "less, he gives play to these impulses of sense "only so far as they do not stand in the way of "the expansion of the higher powers, we are "compelled to call it a moral mode of acting, "which cannot be deduced from pity, and which "seems in no respect the moral attitude of the "man to others, but entirely one to himself."* But whence does the young man derive the power to offer successful resistance to the dominating instincts of the senses? The impulses are no more than the consequence and expression of the necessities; the stronger instinct corresponds with the stronger necessity and conversely. It would seem, therefore, as if a being who was purely the product of necessity, could

---

* P. 235, Sechst. Aufl. 240.

only be determined and guided in his entire conduct by what happens at the time to be the stronger instinct. Or are we after all to suppose that this is a freedom of will, a power of self-determination, sufficiently strong to impose restraint on the different impulses, to hold them, as it were, in check, and to decide for itself by which of them its activities shall be controlled, or whether it shall be controlled by them at all? Yes, is the reply of STRAUSS, there is such a thing as freedom of will. For "all the moral "activity of man is a self-determining of the in- "dividual in accordance with the generic idea "of the race. First of all to actualize this in "himself, to shape and keep the individual in "conformity with the true notion and destina- "tion of humanity, is the sum and substance of "man's duty toward himself. Effectively to "recognize and to advance, in others, our race, "which in itself is equal, is the sum of our du- "ties to others, in which we are to distinguish "between the negative duty, which forbids us to "do anything in prejudice of the equal rights "of any one, and the positive duty of aiding "every one to the extent of our ability—in a "word, between the duties of justice and the "duties of love."* Man, then, not only pos-

---

* P. 236, Sechst. Aufl. 241.

sesses the faculty of self-determination, but he *ought* "to determine himself in accordance with the idea of his race." STRAUSS proclaims, therefore, without further argument, the doctrine of the freedom of the will, that much-contested doctrine, which is denied in downright terms, especially by the whole body of Sensualists and Materialists, which is in general sympathy with his views. With it he proclaims the imperative Shall of the moral law. But apart from every other consideration, such proclamations are, in their own nature, thoroughly unscientific. Science cannot and dare not allow any man, not even so distinguished a man as STRAUSS, to decide a question of scientific controversy with a *sic volo, sic jubeo*—so I will, so I command. If STRAUSS desired to put in a word on this point, he was bound to take hold of the freedom of the will as a problem, and to present his reasons if he felt himself compelled to affirm it. He saves himself the trouble of doing anything of the sort. He decides the question without even telling us how this decision is to be brought into unison with his own premises and fundamental views. And yet it is a manifest contradiction in the adjective to impute the faculty of self-determination to a being "absolutely dependent" on nature. It is just as manifest a contradiction to take a creature of blind natural necessity and of its laws, a mechanism built up and artificially held together by physical and chemical forces, the product of the development of natural necessities and of the instincts set in play by them, and endow such a creature with an "idea of its race," and with a "destination," which the entire kind, and every individual in it, is "bound in duty" to fulfil. Darwinism, indeed, knows nothing of either race or species; it expressly denies the existence of definite genera distinguished by permanent types, involving essential determinations. The originated "living substances" have, indeed, according to Darwinism, in the so-called "Atavism," to hold fast to the innate bias, the parental type; but in the "variability" the equally original adverse bias has to deviate from this type, and consequently from the idea of the race. Both factors are arrayed against each other with entirely equal claims, or rather the second factor, the impulse of variation, of individualizing, has on its side the claim of necessity, the war-claim of the struggle for existence, the supremest claim which Darwinism recognizes. If, then, we grant that the individual can make a decision one way or the other, why should he be bound in duty to repudiate his individuality, and sacrifice his individual instincts, desires, and passions in favor of Atavism? About all such questions STRAUSS gives himself no concern. He never even tells us in what his idea of humanity consists. He talks about the destination of man, but never defines it. Not until he has reached a later point, and then only, in passing, does he make the remark that, by the destination of humanity nothing more can be meant than "the harmonious expansion of man's natural predispositions and capacities."* But he again fails to see that it still remains necessary to show how a being who consists of a physico-chemical combination of atoms, which are the original and sole *supporters* of all his natural predispositions and capacities, can possibly be in a condition, by his actions, to contribute in the slightest measure to "the harmo-"nious expansion of these capacities and pre-"dispositions," either by restraining them or by giving them more strength. In the very nature of the case it is clear, that if a machine is not so constructed that from the very beginning, and of necessity, its parts co-work in harmony, no one particular wheel, no single screw or spring—and consequently, by parity of reason,

---

* P. 263, Sechst. Aufl. 269.

no single part of the brain or nervous system—can produce the lacking harmony, or restore it if it be destroyed. A machine with self-determination and moral obligation is so manifest a contradiction in the adjective, that no man who is unwilling to talk of wooden iron will venture to talk of such a machine.

XXV.

STRAUSS'S ATTEMPT TO SHOW THAT HE DOES NOT HOLD THAT THE UNIVERSE IS A THING OF CHANCE.

To all this we may suppose STRAUSS to reply that it is not his view that the universe is a mere machine, a product of blind chance; that he has explicitly declared that nothing which we perceive in and about us, nothing which we and others experience, is "an isolated fragment, a "wild chaos of atoms or accidents, but that all "proceeds according to eternal laws from the "one primal source of all life, of all reason and "all good;" that consequently reason is to be imputed to man, and that his whole life, acts and conduct should be conformed to it. STRAUSS has undoubtedly asserted all this.* But he has nowhere shown us how this is to be brought

---

* See p. 239, Sechst. Aufl. 244, and in other passages.

into unison with the "blind" force of nature, which not only rules in the inorganic world, but has brought forth the first germs of life by a physical chemical mingling of atoms, and under the autocracy of blind necessity has developed them into mankind. We are compelled to ask, therefore, What is this reason? in what way does it work? and how is it to be distinguished from the rule of blind chance? As we have shown that the "delicate, mild, tender," cannot, without more proof than has been adduced, be identified with the good and rational, there remains for the reason which rules in the world, no other notion than that of necessity and conformity with law. On this then STRAUSS ultimately falls back at the "conclusion" of his discussions, where he again has occasion to speak of his new faith. He there says:* "Our God (the universe) shows us in-"deed that chance would be an irrational ruler "of the world, but that necessity, that is, the con-"catenation of causes in the world, is reason it-"self." Why the concatenation of causes in the world is coincident with reason, in what respect this necessity is rational, we are as remote from learning, as we were at the earlier proclamation

---

* P. 365, Sechst. Aufl 372.

that the rational is the delicate and tender, and yet it is manifestly by no means necessary that all necessity as such, that every concatenation of causes should also be rational, that an irrational concatenation should be impossible. At all events this "necessity" is and remains a "blind" power of nature. For that a spiritual, conscious power controls the world and concatenates the causes, the operative forces, is denied and contested by STRAUSS from the beginning of his book to the end of it. The reason for which he argues distinguishes itself from chance, therefore, by being blind necessity, while chance is usually designated as blind caprice; the latter might also, though but fortuitously, have brought forth the delicate and tender, beside the coarse and harsh. But what does it matter whether blind necessity or blind caprice, with reason or without reason, concatenates the forces which work in nature? If man be "absolutely dependent" on them and their concatenation, we cannot speak of self-determination or freedom, of rational or irrational decisions of the will. On the contrary, blind caprice might have endowed yet earlier the being it brought forth with a power of capricious volition and working, resembling itself; the dominion of blind necessity absolutely excludes everything suggestive of caprice, freedom, self-determination. STRAUSS's view therefore stands fast by the wooden iron of a being who is "absolutely dependent," and yet "self-determining."

XXVI.

NATURE COMING TO SELF-RECOGNITION.

But STRAUSS goes yet further. In what follows he not only ascribes reason to this blindly working necessity, but also attributes to it will, and that, too, a will to recognize itself! He begins with citing a judgment expressed by MORIZ WAGNER, that "the most important general re-"sult revealed to us by comparative geology "and palæontology is the great law of progress "which rules in nature. From the most ancient "eras of the history of the earth, which have "left traces of organic life, down to creation as "it is at present, this steady progress in the ap-"pearing of more highly organized beings than "those of the past is a fact firmly established by "experience; and this fact is perhaps the most "consolatory of all the truths which science has "ever attained." STRAUSS then goes on to say: "In this ascending movement of life man also "is embraced, and in such a way that in him "the organic plastic force on our planet has

"reached its climax. As it cannot go further,
"cannot go beyond itself, it will enter into
"itself. HEGEL's expression—reflecting self in
"self—was a thoroughly good one. In the
"animal, nature had a sensation of herself: but
"she wills also to have recognition of herself."*
An astounding declaration! Blindly working
unconscious nature, with her Reason destitute of
personality and consciousness, unable to go
further, to go beyond herself, enters into herself,
in order to attain self-recognition, and by this
means to reach at last consciousness and self-
knowledge! But how does nature come to take
such an extraordinary fancy? What is to prevent her going "further" beyond herself, inasmuch as the great law of progress proves that
she is quite able to go "beyond herself?" And
above all—this boundless plurality of atoms of
which nature consists, and in the unceasing alternation of the combinations and separations
of which she produces and reproduces herself—
how does it come to pass that it " enters into itself, to reflect itself in itself?" Can an atom
of hydrogen, oxygen, or carbon, or any mass of
them, combine them as you will, reflect itself in
itself? Is not this reflection in itself an activity

---

* P. 240, Sechst. Aufl. 244, 245.

NATURE COMING TO SELF-RECOGNITION. 157

which can be put forth only by a being with soul, or intellect, a being bearing a "Self" in itself? STRAUSS, as we have seen, has pronounced thoroughly unnatural a self-conscious rule of nature, acting in accordance with plan and design, and has lauded DARWIN as the greatest benefactor of mankind, for setting aside forever the notion of design in this sense. And now we have nature creating man, and in him reflecting herself in herself, so that in him she may recognize herself! But if Nature ever adopted this unnatural determination, and if she really had the power of creating man, in order to execute her will through him, in his recognition of Self and of Nature, would it not have been more accordant with her design, as well as a shorter and simpler way, instead of making this wide circuit, to have reflected herself at once in herself, and thus have reached the desired self-recognition at the outstart? For what good would she derive from this trailing self-recognition, embracing as it would her doing and her working only when it was too late—after everything was finished? Is not this style of proceeding irrational? And this blindly swaying Nature, which knows nothing and recognizes nothing, and yet is striving after self-recognition, does it not come again into the category of the wooden iron?

XXVII.

STRAUSS'S DIRECT CONTRADICTION OF HIMSELF.

STRAUSS has so little dread of the contradictory, that not satisfied with the indirect and implicit, he involves himself in the most direct and express self-contradictions. Thus, for example, we first find him teaching us that nature, after her organic plastic force has reached, in man, its climax, " could go no further, beyond herself," and consequently entered into herself. But on the next page he asserts* that " in man " nature has not merely in a general way willed " upwards, but has willed out beyond herself; " man, therefore, should not only not relapse " into the animal, he should be more, he should " be something better." Nature, consequently, though she *could* not go further, beyond herself, has at least *willed* out beyond herself. In fact, she has not merely willed it, but has made the impossible possible. For man exists, and he

---

* P. 241, Sechst. Aufl. 246.

not only "should" and "can" be more than a mere animal over again, but the man of moral standing and moral conduct *is* more. It is true he cannot totally avoid " the rough, hard struggle for existence" which in the animal kingdom had already had such an abundant sway: "So "far he is still a being of nature, but he ought "to know how to ennoble and soften the strug-"gle in accordance with the measure of his "higher faculties." Man is consequently no longer a mere "being of nature," he has "higher" faculties, in the harmonious expansion of which, and by the embodiment of which in his actions, he exalts himself *above* nature. Nature has then, in fact, succeeded in finally passing out beyond herself; she has succeeded in getting loose from herself, in reaching out beyond herself, beyond her own measure, her own strength, her own essential nature. She has succeeded, consequently, in becoming *supernatural*. In brief, she has brought to a happy issue the seemingly impossible feat of leaping away from herself. She has jumped out of her skin! If she be capable of such performances, we no longer wonder that she is capable of contradicting herself, and that she cannot only will and do contradictory things, but is able to think them.

XXVIII.

STRAUSS'S IDEAL STRIVINGS. HIS RECOGNITION OF MYSTERY.

After man has been thus hypostatized into a being half natural, half supernatural, or a being "yet" natural, though supernatural, we need scarcely wonder longer that STRAUSS speaks of "ideal strivings,"* that he maintains that by "the giving of the higher position to the indi-"vidual with his material necessities and de-"mands, the loftier interests, the interests of "the spirit are imperilled,"† and that he decidedly disapproves of "the direction which by "pre-eminence both science and education take "in America toward the exact and practical, "the serviceable and the utilitarian." In his charming zeal for science and art he forgets that for Darwinists and Materialists there can be absolutely no ideal strivings, no higher intellectual "interests" overbalancing the material necessities and demands, no science which does not ask after the serviceable and the utilitarian. His forgetfulness indeed extends so far that in defending the monarchial constitution against

---

* P. 259.
† P. 265, Sechst. Aufl. 270, 271.

the republicans, he enunciates the proposition: "Every mystery seems absurd, and yet there is "nothing profound, neither life, nor art, nor "state, without mystery." We attach great value to such instances of self-forgetfulness on the part of STRAUSS as a man, but considering them as the words of STRAUSS the philosophical thinker, the harbinger of the faith of the future, we cannot allow them to pass without reminding him that the proposition to which he has committed himself involves the best defence of religion in general, and of Christianity in particular, and breaks the point of his arguments against the old faith. If there be nothing profound without mystery, it is difficult to see why religion, the profoundest thing to which man is able to attain, and especially the Christian religion, should be made exceptions, and the mystery which surrounds them be urged to their disadvantage, and made a reason for their extirpation. Even the God of the new faith, the Universe, as the primal source of all reason and of all good, still bears in its bosom, as we have shown, very much that is mysterious, unexplained, and uncomprehended. But should STRAUSS propose to distinguish between mystery and mystery, to grant one kind and repudiate another, he must be able to furnish a safe criterion for the separation of the true mystery from the false one. Or are we to suppose that there are grades of the mysterious, so that when it passes beyond a certain measure it is no longer to be tolerated? This does not seem to be STRAUSS's view. For the last bound of all the mystical is the contradictory, and it is this precise bound beyond which, as we have seen, STRAUSS passes only too often.

XXIX.

CONCLUSION. THE NEW PHILOSOPHY.

The two "Supplements" which STRAUSS has added, bearing the titles, "Our Great Poets" and "Our Great Musicians," do not fall within the province of this notice. We do not propose, in the slightest degree, to disturb him in his æsthetic enjoyment, which to him supplies preeminently the place of religious edification; we are not going to call into doubt his high æsthetic culture; we see no reason for depreciating his æsthetic judgment, which, indeed, we consider entirely sound, and which furnishes new evidence of his profoundly ethical nature. Still even here it is once more wholly incomprehensible how, in pure beauty, that thoroughly useless, unserviceable thing, the Darwinian man, can find such a cordial, inspiring delight! Nor shall we go on to demonstrate—a thing very easy to do—that the "compensation" which the new religion pretends to furnish for the vanished consolations of the old religion, for the assurance of reconciliation with God, for faith in Providence, for the hope of a loftier and better being, the compensation which STRAUSS* proffers us at the close of his book is in truth no compensation at all. We are concerned here, not with STRAUSS as critic, either æsthetical or theological, not with STRAUSS as dogmatician, or as a teacher of religion, but *simply* with STRAUSS as a philosophical thinker. And of STRAUSS in that aspect we believe we have sufficiently shown that his new philosophy, for even it is new as contrasted with the philosophy of his earlier view of the world, is no philosophy at all, inasmuch as it is the persistent carrying through of a renunciation of all logic.

---

* P. 364 seq. Sechst. Aufl. 370 seq.

INDEX.

Adam, 46
Agassiz, 16, 51
America, 38, 51, 160
Animals, 125
Ape, 45, 46, 125, 128
Aristotle, 15, 22, 51
Atavism, 150
Atheism, 50, 56, 78
Atoms, 131

Baader, 49
Bad, 103
Baer, von, 52
Barnard, 53, 54
Beyschlag, 40
Biela's comet, 113
Bismarck, 58, 59
Bohner, 31
Bronn, 53
Büchner, 31, 54

Carrière, 36, 48
Carus, 53
Casualist, 102
Causality, 81-84
    notion and mental law of, 87
Chance, 103
Child, 81
Christ, 50
Christianity, 45
Christians, 43, 78
Clausius, 52
Comets, 113
Comte, 19

Conscience, 126
Contradictions in the adjective, 89, 93, 108, 111, 142
Cuvier, 51
Czolbe, 53

Darwin, 16, 90, 120-123, 137, 138, 143, 157
Darwinian theory, Darwinism, 24, 45, 120, 122, 125, 139-143, 150, 162
Des Cartes, 22
Descendence, 125
Diderot, 21, 46
Discovery, 100
Discussions, 31
Dog, 126
Donders, 52, 56, 130
Dove, 37, 42
Du Bois-Reymond, 52, 56, 131, 133-136

Earth, 110
Eisenlohr, 51, 123, 124
Eleatics, 109
Encke's comet, 114
Epictetus, 41
Epicureans, 94
Erdmann, 27

Fabri, 31
Faith, the new, 33, 34, 74, 98
Fear, 80-83

INDEX.

Fechner, 52
Feuerbach, 31, 41, 42, 93
Fichte, 1, 4, 22, 31, 37, 40, 48, 49, 71
Finite, 111
Freedom, 105
Frenzel, 37, 40, 45
Frohschammer, 31, 37, 47

Generatio æquivoca, 116
Goethe, 58, 60, 61
Good, 104
Gravitation, 123
Greeks, 84

Haeckel, 53
Hartmann, von, 41, 106, 137
Hausrath, 37, 41
Hegel, 22, 49, 71
Helmholtz, 16, 22, 52, 129
Herbart, 49
Huber, 36, 49, 124
Humboldt, 16, 58
Hume, 41
Huxley, 54

Incarnation, 128
Inconsistency, 49
Infinite, 108
Inorganic, 116
Instincts, 126
Interest, points of, 39
Introduction, 72

Jesus, 44, 50, 61

Kant, 22, 41, 51, 52, 113
Kekulé, 123
Knoodt, 36
Koelliker, 53
Krause, 49

Lamarck, 51

La Mettrie, 21
Laplace, 51, 113
Lang, H., 64
Lang, W., 40
Lazarus, 49
Leibnitz, 22
Lessing, 60
Lewes, 19
Liebig, 51
Life, 116
Living substances, 116–120
Logic, 99, 163
Lotze, 16, 22, 48, 49, 71
Luther, 61
Lyell, 117

Mariana, 38
Materialism, 9, 13, 23, 25, 27, 30, 78, 106, 128
Materialists, 103, 106
Mazzini, 63
Metaphysics, 17
Metempyrics, 20
Meyer, J. B., 37
Michelis, 36, 41
Miracles, 121
Mischievous tendencies, 58
Moleschott, 31, 47
Monotheism, 84
Morality, 105
Müller, J., 51, 52
Munchausen, 89
Mystery, 161

Nägele, 53
Natural theology, 57
Nature, 159
New England, 25
Newton, 51, 123
Nippold, 37, 38, 39, 71

Oken, 51
Optimism, 107
Organic, 115

INDEX. 167

Pascal, 22
People, 62
Pessimism, 106
Philosophical spirit, 18
Philosophy, 163
Phillipson, 33, 37, 40, 41
Physicists, 22
Planck, 53
Political elements, 63
Polytheism, 84
Positivism, 19
Priestcraft, 48

Rational, 102
Rauwenhoff, 38, 39, 58, 64, 66
Reactionary tendency, 65
Reimarus, 51
Religion, 11, 79–95
Reviewers, 35
Ritter, 49
Rome, 66

Schaller, 22, 31
Schelling, 22, 49
Schleiden, 53
Schleiermacher, 93
Scholten, 38, 53
Schopenhauer, 26, 41, 66, 106, 147
Science, 10
Sensation, 128
Sensualism, 128
Smith, H. B, 38
Snell, 53
Solar systems, 110
Soul, 128
Species, 120
Spörri, 37, 65
Sterling, 58
Strauss, 14, 28, 29, 31, 32, 35, 69, 73, 75, 79, 89–98, 115–137, 162
Stutz, 38
Supernatural, 12, 149

Teleology, 90, 137, 139
Theism, 68
Tittmann, 31
Trendlenburg, 49, 71
Trinity, 100
Tyndall, 16, 33, 55

Ulrici, 14, 22, 29, 31, 49, 56, 69, 70, 92, 113
Unconscious, 137
Universal, 98, 153

Vera, 38
Vierordt, 53
Virchow, 116
Vogt, 31, 41, 45, 47
Voltaire, 41, 46
Von Holbach, 21

Wagner, M., 155
Wagner, R., 51
Warmth, 129
"We," 45, 75, 100
Weis, 37
Weisse, 48, 49
Will, 103
Wirth, 49
World, 109
Wundt, 53

Ziegler, 38
Zierngebel, 36

WORKS OF DR. KRAUTH.

FOR SALE BY SMITH, ENGLISH & CO.

Strauss as a Philosophical Thinker.
From the German of ULRICI. With an Introduction. 12mo. 1874, ... $1.00

Berkeley's Principles of Human Knowledge.
With Prolegomena and Annotations. 8vo. 1874, $3 50

The Conservative Reformation and its Theology.
8vo., pp. 858. 1871, ... $5.00

The Vocabulary of Philosophy.
By FLEMING. With an Introduction, Chronology, Bibliographical Index, Synthetical Tables, and other Additions. Second Edition. 12mo., pp. 686. 1873, . $2.50

Tholuck's Commentary on John.
Translated from the Sixth and Seventh Editions. 8vo. 1872, ... $3.00

www.ingramcontent.com/pod-product-compliance
Lightning Source LLC
Chambersburg PA
CBHW030252170426
43202CB00009B/710